BORN INTO CRAZY

by Diana Heldenbrand

PROLOGUE

This story is based on real events. This is written from the perspective of a child living with a parent, diagnosed with a severe mental illness. It is a coming of age story about addiction, mental illness, abuse, healing, family, and forgiveness. It shows the viewpoint of a child getting caught in the chaos, pain, and confusion of mental illness.

Writing this was cathartic and painful. It forced me to confront feelings, accept harsh truths, and grieve the reality of the losses experienced. It also helped me to appreciate the gifts that the past provided and helped me to gain deeper compassion for my mother and her illness. I got to know myself and my family very well in reflecting on my life.

In the 23 years since I left home, I have confronted my feelings about my mother's schizoaffective diagnosis and accepted the experiences of my unusual

childhood.

The complexity, shame, loss, anger, and difficulty

of living with mental illness is not easy, especially for

children. It has taken time and reflection for me to get to a

place of freedom. Showing my scars no longer feels

frightening. I no longer need to hide my truth. This crazy,

painful, tragic, and beautiful life - is a painting with a

thousand strokes and varied colors that don't always match

perfectly alongside each other. The painting that is my life

is both beautiful and ugly, and this is my story.

CHAPTER 1 - MOM

It was 1988 and I was seven when I discovered mom had a mental illness. Mom had gone missing. She left the house in a quiet and undramatic exit. She had nothing with her and walked out the front door. I was a child, left alone. I called my grandparents. "She left", I told them. "Where did she go?" my grandma demanded. "I don't know, she just left." They came to get me that winter evening. A day came and went, the temperature dropped, and mom had still not returned. My grandparents began calling all the local hospitals, jails, and morgues. They called mom's friends, and family members, including extended. They visited the local homeless shelters. No one had seen her, she simply vanished. Family members missed work to search for her. I was worried sick, and the worst parts of my imagination began to go wild. Where could she be? Was she alive?

She left in shorts and sandals in sub-zero temperatures in Iowa, that cold winter day. She left her keys and coat and took off walking in the snow with little on. A week went by and nothing. One week turned into two weeks, and *still,* no one had seen or heard from her. At three weeks missing, we were all very worried because the Iowa weather was taking a frigid turn. It was an exceptionally cold winter in Iowa, and we knew that frostbite or even death were a real possibility. By this point, the family was putting up flyers and reaching out to the community to help find her. My grandparents were calling anyone who would listen.

While I slept next to my grandmother one night, we heard glass break in the darkness. It was her. Mom broke the glass out of their bedroom window and crashed onto the floor. She had come for me, to take me in the night. She had been gone for a long time, and now she demanded to have me back as if no time had passed. That's how it was with her. Like an unstable chameleon, one minute she was there and the next she was not. She came in with a dramatic entrance. A struggle ensued and I remember her hitting my grandpa. "You leave now or else I'll call the police", he said with the softest tone. Grandpa was the kindest and most gentle man, and he had no brutality in him at all. It's odd to imagine him in his WWII days, being in a war because he possessed such a gentle soul with awe-inspiring patience. She loved fighting. She provoked him, yelling "Do it!" and

"You stole my kid!" Her logic was impaired and there was no ability to reason with her.

Mom had a tendency for provoking people to fight and was relentless until they joined in her insanity. She would become physically violent and then play the victim once the scene changed. Grandpa always knew the best response was no response, and he gave her no reaction at all. In this way, he never provided ammunition for a battle to occur.

Before the cops arrived that night, she left on foot. That was my life, never knowing what the next day would bring.

It was a month before we found her. The strangers who found her heard a strange sound in their home and went downstairs to investigate the noise. They were shocked and struck with fear at seeing a shivering and nearly incoherent person huddled in the center of their ice-cold basement. They didn't know this woman, and she didn't know them. They observed her talking to herself, and she seemed incoherent.

The police arrived and took mom to the mental hospital. To this day, our family doesn't know where she disappears when she goes missing. During this particular episode, we are still unsure where she had been for that entire missing month. Later, when her mind came back, she was irate that we would dare look for her and put the word out publicly that she was gone. "I'm an adult and I can come and go as I like," she said. "If I wanted you to find me, I'd let you." Her mind didn't understand that leaving a child and disappearing for a month might be cause for alarm to her family.

My grandparents tried to keep me away from the reality that was my mother's mental illness. "She's sick honey," they would tell me. My grandmother coped tremendously with codependency and denial. She had the "fixer" mentality and believed that her willpower alone could fix any problem. At the end of the day, all of grandma's stubborn attempts to cure mom didn't remedy her mental illness. Her interference exacerbated the problem. I liken curing mom's illness to trying to tear down a mountain with a spatula. Some issues require so much more power and effort than one person could attempt to provide.

My family has never really acknowledged how sick mom is. I often wondered what the catalyst to her illness was. She experienced a lot of trauma at a young age. She lost a brother to a freak accident at age 27. Many family members struggled with addiction and drugs. There were two fires, tragic deaths, and illnesses, but none of this ever revealed a weakness in my grandparent's character or resolve. They simply had no visible crakes to their strength. However, mom often fell apart.

Mom started doing drugs at age eleven and being sexually promiscuous at a young age. Grandma dealt with her daughter the way she dealt with every problem. She used her strong will to try to control the mess that was my mother. As much as she pushed her toward a healthier path, she pushed back harder by rebelling more and falling deeper into the hole of drugs and mental illness. They were two very stubborn forces going against each other their entire lives.

When mom was fifteen, her brother died tragically at a young age. During the hours preceding his death, the two of them had a massive argument. Her last words to him were, "I hope you die; I hate you." Of course, she didn't mean it, but he did die just a few short hours after her words were spoken. Then, a few weeks later while in church, she watched her Pastor have a massive heart attack and die in the middle of the service. Not long after, my grandmother forced her to have an abortion. It was a very difficult time in her life and the disruption that was her illness revealed itself.

When mom would go off the mental cliff or go missing, my grandparents often took me into their home to live with them. During her psychotic episodes, the family considered her a harm to herself and others. She would become violent and later she would be unable to recall the events which occurred.

I was an anxious child and developed a form of Alopecia, where large chunks of my hair would fall out due to stress. My stomach would be in knots and fear was a friend. All I thought about was, what will happen today?

CHAPTER 2 – BLOOD ON THE STUCCO HOUSE

When I was eight, mom was in the middle of a "spell", as our family would come to call it. No one liked to use the term mentally ill, so they called it a "spell". This became the expression my family used to describe her illness, as it was seen to be less stigmatic.

It began on a hot day when all the neighborhood kids were playing in my back yard. My grandpa bought a used swing set and had recently brought it to our house. My grandparents purchased a home for us when their son died. Mom was unfit to work. They tried to make sure we had the essentials. For a time, my backyard was the coolest place to be. On this day, just about every child in our neighborhood was taking turns on my new but used swing set.

Our house was a small, two-bedroom, stucco home built in the 1920s. We had two large mulberry trees that covered our yard in a purple mush. One of the children who lived on the corner of our block jumped over my fence. He said he could hear mom yelling for me around the side of the house. He had been picking mulberries off our tree and his hands were purple as he approached. I jumped off the swing and walked to the side of the house. As I walked down the driveway, that's when I saw it. There was blood running down the stucco, forming a pool in the chipped gravel. There was broken glass scattered everywhere. My eyes followed the trail of blood and I saw her face sticking through the shattered bathroom window. Blood was dripping from her chin down the side of the house. The thick blood made her barely recognizable. At first, I wasn't sure exactly what I was looking at. Her appearance shocked me into a frozen state. Standing behind her was a tall heavyset man with wild black curly hair and an and unruly beard. He was tall, very muscular, and exceptionally cruel. His hands were wrapped tightly around mom's neck, while she gurgled and struggled to call my name. He had a sick look of pleasure on his twisted face as he stood behind her. While he strangled her, I noticed the shards of glass protruding from her face and the blood seemed to paint the front of her shirt a bright red. It felt like my feet were stuck and I couldn't move. Shock took over my body and my heart began to race faster than my lungs could keep up. I lost sight of where I was and what was happening around me. The laughter of the children playing on the swing set faded, and my heart began to throb, a deep pounding in my ears. It felt like minutes passed, as I stood there unable to breathe or move. Suddenly, my neighbor Cathy swooped me up into her arms and carried me away from the violent scene. I was sobbing and I didn't even know it.

I watched out Cathy's window as six police cars surrounded our small stucco house. I heard screaming and the sounds of shots being fired. All the neighbors were watching this scene unfold like a Jerry Springer show, but this was my *real* life, not something for entertainment. I watched as they finally got him down to the ground. Four cops attempted to pin him while crawling on top of him, forcing him into handcuffs. He didn't go down without a fight. I watched as they took him away in a patrol car, the loud sounds got further away just as my heart-beat finally started to slow down and my mind came back from the dream to my reality.

Mom was taken to the emergency room, while I stayed with my neighbor Cathy. Mom ended up getting seven stitches on her right eyelid. The doctor said, had the glass cut her just a few more millimeters, then she would have been permanently blinded.

I hated that she liked this excitement. It made a dull life somehow interesting; it made her *feel* something inside. She liked the thrill and the attention that crazy brought to her life. Even if she couldn't help the chemical imbalance in her brain, I knew she loved it and I despised that fact.

Mom returned and once the blood was washed away, all that remained were a few cuts and stitches and she looked like her normal self. I was glad to see her white, freckled, familiar face again. Both she and Cathy were never quiet in their gossipy conversations about Dane, and I often listened to every detail, sometimes stealing sips of mom's coffee. I was afraid and wanted to gain knowledge in order to feel more powerful as a child so that I could know what to expect so I eavesdropped.

Mom wanted to go out and was getting ready. She had been washing her hair in the bathtub, and in a jealous rage, he held her face under the water, trying to drown her. She was beautiful and he was jealous. He didn't like the outfit she was wearing and hated her receiving any form of attention. His violence was without warning. She fought him off and they struggled. He was well over six feet and she was only five feet even so she never stood a chance with him physically. Gaining control, he pushed her face out of the glass bathroom window, shattering the glass and cutting her face. She had been screaming my name and managed to get out a few solid screams before he began strangling her. He was a very violent man, who was even more violent when he drank, which was most days.

Dane was taken to the county jail and held on bail. This incident ended up throwing mom off balance and she began acting erratically soon after. Before anyone else could ever see her escalate into a "spell", I was always the person to see it coming first. I learned very young to analyze her and read her every action, thought, tone, expression, and behavior. It's hard to explain, but it's a slight series of noticeable changes. First, I notice that she stops looking at people directly in the eye and becomes fidgety. She lets out weird laughs at inappropriate times. Then she stops sleeping. The lack of sleep causes her brain to shut down. Not soon after, she stops making sense in her conversation. Then she will talk to herself and have full-blown conversations that don't make any logical sense to a sane brain. Next, come the paranoia and delusions. When it gets to that point, it begins to get scary because what follows is either disappearance or violence. The family tries to get her help as early in the process as possible, so she cannot hurt others or herself.

I knew she was off when she insisted that Cathy drive her to the jail and tried to climb the jail building. This was just one day after Dane was arrested for trying to kill her. He literally just tried to drown her and shoved her face through a glass window, yet here she was shouting his name outside the jail. She screamed his name at the top of her lungs, convinced he would somehow hear her through the brick walls. None of it made sense. People passed by with their typical stares in reaction to her crazy ways. I was used to the faces of judgment that my mom's mental illness drew to us. She attracted judgment like bees to honey. People couldn't help but watch the train wreck and I suppose it was entertainment for them. Embarrassment and shame were constants for me. I dealt with it by turning inward. No one could reach me inside and I stayed in silence. I was an extremely shy, awkward, and withdrawn child. There were parts of myself which no one ever saw, especially mom. I later discovered that shutting myself off was actually something called dissociation, and it became a means of survival. I went to great lengths to protect myself and I found silence and hiding to be my best forms of protection. I also learned to turn off my emotions and not react. She would use any vulnerabilities against me so I learned to live deeply hidden within myself.

Mom somehow managed to get the money to post a bond for Dane's release. My grandparents signed the house to her, and she used her house as collateral. I begged her in tears not to do this. "He's going to kill you," I pleaded. I was convinced and terrified he would kill us both. We lived in a house of threats; a house of fears and horrors. I didn't hesitate once that he was capable of murder. Of course, she didn't listen. She never listened.

CHAPTER 3 – HIDING IN THE ATTIC

Mom posted bail so Dane could get released, which was a very large amount of money. Driving home from the jail, he immediately began to rant, telling her to stop to buy him some liquor. He was clearly jonesing. Drugs and alcohol were how he dealt with stress in life. She told him that she would not be stopping. I remember his quick and hostile escalation to a red-faced monster lurching toward her. His face twisted into that of a demon. With no hesitancy, he reached over lifting her shirt, to reveal her breasts. Mom had very large breasts and I watched horrified as he dug his fingernails deep into the skin, twisting and pinching around her nipple until she cried begging him to stop. She pulled over the car, unable to drive because he had her breast so tightly twisted in his firm grip. She could barely breathe, talk, or cry. Years later, I would flinch at my husband's touch as the memory of this moment would return to me.

We were parked at a gas station near the Iowa State Fairgrounds on University and 30th, and on-goers were watching as he blatantly abused her publicly. He saw nothing wrong with hurting women and had absolutely no hesitation about doing it visibly. It baffled me how strangers could watch something like this happen and manage to laugh or joke. I could hear their judgmental thoughts and sometimes brutally honest comments which they shared aloud, "They're a mess!", "Glad it's not us.", "White trash!" I saw eyes roll, people flee, giggles, snickers, and stares. I hated being in that situation, and I hated people's response to it. The shame, fear, and embarrassment made me want to disappear.

I could see the torture he was inflicting. Being so immersed in fear, I couldn't turn away. I felt scared and helpless. "Get me a drink," he shouted. She always resisted. This stubborn, power playing, sadistic game continued. Fear gripped my entire body. Sensing her hesitancy, he twisted her breast harder and harder until the color began to turn from white to a reddish-purple. She began to bleed, and by this point, I was sobbing, and she was crying out in pains of yelping and howling. Finally, she raised the white flag and responded with a defeated nod. He had won and she was awarded a smug satisfied expression.

Down the road from the gas station, near our home, was a liquor store. It's always interesting to me how they put places like that in the worst neighborhoods possible.

Most of the people who worked there were good friends with mom. Mom purchased a bottle of vodka from the liquor store and she got the strongest alcohol she could find for herself as well as a pack of cigarettes. The smell of the cheap menthol cigarettes often bothered my throat. We were only a few blocks from home when he began swallowing large gulps of alcohol.

I already knew what was coming that night. His devil came almost every night, but especially on the nights that he drank. As expected, his anger raged on heavily. He was a high functioning drunk in that he never passed out. He just seemed to get angrier and angrier as he drank turning homicidal. He drank rapidly and it seemed his tolerance to liquor made him have to drink more to feel more intoxicated.

As the screams got louder, I hid inside my room. I heard crashing sounds coming from the living room. I heard bodies slamming, glass breaking, and voices screaming. Amidst all the crashes, there were violent screams going between the two of them. Usually, she begged him to stop and he inflicted some form of torturous abuse upon her. I would always be pulled into the middle of their fights. He never failed to mention my name and I would get dragged out in the center of their wars and battles. He mentioned being severely abused as a child and he had a deep hatred for children. Being cruel was as normal to him as getting dressed every day.

I grabbed a blanket and climbed into the attic. The attic was accessible from my bedroom. My room was small with pink painted chipped walls and a pink panther poster, which my grandma got for me. Grandma also bought me a small Winnie the pooh lamp which I quickly turned off. Pink Panther was one of my favorite cartoons to watch with my grandparents. We especially liked all the old cartoons like The Flintstones, Jetsons, Pink Panther, and Yogi Bear but my absolute favorite was Pink Panther. In my bedroom, I didn't have carpet, blinds, or sheets on my bed, but I did have a blanket, which my aunt had handmade for me. It was my favorite color, pink. I told her that I liked the one she made for my cousin, so she made me a blanket also. It was a great comfort to me, during chaotic moments such as these. Recently, mom told me I would be getting a waterbed and she brought a large wooden box in my room. It looked like someone hand made a giant box. I never ended up getting the water mattress, so I slept in the empty wooden box. Friends who would come over thought this was very strange.

The vile noises of crashing and screaming continued as I made my way into the attic above my bedroom. It was a bit colder and you could often hear the rain pouring louder in the confined space. It was small and a place intended for storage, but I crawled there often to escape the noise. There was always so much noise. There was never a quiet moment and all the fighting set my nerves on edge.

In that moment, I began asking God to make this end. I heard Dane push her against the wall and her breath let out in a pained exhale. Next, it sounded as if he pushed over the piano. My grandfather paid for piano lessons and music became another means of escape. Grandpa found this piano in wanted ads and got it for under $100. The piano was out of tune, three black keys stuck, and it had chipped paint, but I absolutely loved it. Like every young girl wants a pony, I wanted a piano and I treasured it. Playing that piano would take me away to another place. I usually played over the noise. They didn't hear me banging on the keys against their sounds, and I pretended to not hear them over my heavy fingers.

They struggled down the hallway, past the bathroom, toward my bedroom and I could hear them getting closer. As they approached, in a sharp tone, he shouted my name. His large body was stumbling against the hallway walls. She continued to fight him off. He said, "I saw the bitch take your money." He often accused me of things I didn't do so he would have an excuse to abuse me. Once he accused me of smoking one of mom's cigarettes. Mom believed him and tried to get me to smoke in front of her. She pushed me for a long time to take a drag, which I refused to do. He took off my pants and began to beat me with a board in our front yard. He liked people to see the humiliation when he disciplined me.

In the attic, I was hunkered down, motionless. They both found it weird that I would hide in various places, especially the attic. Hiding always made me feel safe. In the attic, we had mice very badly and I could feel the mice turds under my feet as I tried to sit still and not make a sound. I was a little worried that a mouse might run across my feet but more worried about the monster approaching my room. The smell of the attic was a mixture of dampness, mold, dust, and animal feces. We often lost pets in our home, including a gerbil and a cat. The paint was peeling and there were pieces of pink insulation. But I preferred that smell over violence.

I knew if he found me, he would send me into the cold basement. He might make me take off all my clothes or make me put my face against the cold cement. He might make me stand on my head for a long period. He always came up with creative ways of inflicting pain. One of the cruelest of these was when he forced my head into a hole in the basement wall. I was petrified of centipedes and would frequently find them in our basement, along with garter snakes. He used that fear heavily against me to gain complete control over my fragile mind, saying there were bugs in the hole and that they would crawl on my face. He forced my head inside the hole, while my mom just stood there saying nothing. I sobbed and cried out to her. I hated it when she allowed him to hurt me. Her weakness to him infuriated me.

He had numerous cruel ways to inflict hurt but being alone in a dark basement was the most unendurable for me. He would send me to the basement as a form of punishment. He would come up with lies to send me down there as punishment, but this was to simply get rid of me. The darkness, cold, and isolation were very hard on my sensitive soul. He made sure all the lights and bulbs were gone so I was *forced* to be in the darkness. He made me put my face against the cold cement. We had several rooms in our basement and on the far-left, there was an especially dark room with a cement floor. You had to take a step down to enter the room and when our basement would flood, this room always got the worst of the overflow. It was very damp and cold in this room and it seemed that more bugs existed there. It had concrete walls and no windows. It smelled strong of mildew and mold. This small room is where I would find the creepy crawlers and that is where he would force me to go when I was bad. Sometimes toward the top ledge, there would be holes, where I would see small green striped snakes slithering. I remember sobbing in the dark and being so cold countless times in that basement. As a child, I would train my mind to go to other places so I could temporarily endure this torment. Daydreaming helped me survive.

In the attic, I began to hear two new voices approaching down the hallway. As I sat holding my breath, it became apparent that a fistfight was now transpiring. The sounds of breaking walls, bodies slamming, yells, and hitting, were on full display for my ears to hear. There were men yelling and more than one, I noticed. Everyone in our neighborhood knew of the loud fights and frequent police visits. Sometimes when the fights would get loud, I would hope that a neighbor was listening so the police could be called. They never knew that they were often my source of hope. As the fighting ensued, I was able to pick up on the voice of my uncle. He was very intimidating. He was covered in hair and looked like a bear, hence how he got his nickname Sugar Bear, on the CB radio. I heard him say in his thick voice, "Where is she?" He had the voice of ten men when he spoke. There was a multilayered sound that came out, making him very frightening. Mom replied, "She's not here. She's with a friend." My uncle burst open my bedroom door and I was suddenly surprised to see his face as he opened the attic. He reached for me, taking me into his hairy arms. Like a bear, he was both scary and cuddly. "Come with me", he said. "Quickly." I jumped into his arms as mom began hitting and provoking him. He took me outside of the house and through the back door as my other uncle held her off. The dog followed us to the car and my uncle kicked him away. Our sheltie dog was always by my side until he was hit by a car a few years later. His bones were protruding from his leg, but mom refused to put him down. That night, we quickly got into the car where grandpa was waiting for me with the engine running.

I could feel my heart pounding and feel that I was unable to catch up to my quick breathing. Seeing mom lose control never got any easier over the years and it was hard for my child-mind to comprehend why she was doing this. It took me some time before I understood that her chemical imbalance was nothing which she had any power over. However, in my child-mind, I thought, why can't she try harder? I thought she had power over her illness and simply chose poorly, however now I know better.

CHAPTER 4 – MENTAL ILLNESS

I began to develop panic attacks around the age of eight, along with a mild form of Alopecia, brought on by anxiety and fear. I would lose circle patches of my hair and my stomach was constantly upset from worry. I had digestive issues and struggled in school as well. As a child, it played frequently in my mind that I would be murdered, or mom would be murdered. The only time I can recall feeling safe was when I was with my grandparents and even then, I knew the time with them was a ticking alarm. I couldn't be with them permanently. I would be forced to go back to the crazy house of chaos.

My grandparents didn't just go to church or *say* they were Christians; they lived it in their character. Both were amazingly kind, loving, good parents, and good people. They were the kind of people who baked for their sick friends, visited the nursing homes to encourage lonely residents. Grandpa would volunteer at the hospital and they were always inviting others to holiday dinners. They ran a business and would try to help people who were down and out and unemployed. They were incredible people, on the inside, in their character. Who they were, left an impact on me and I never understood how mom fell so far from that tree. But then again, it was her illness bringing hell to us, not her.

That night, Dane was arrested again for assaulting my mother. Grandpa pulled up to their two-story gray house with the rose bush and barn-like garage. Grandma stood in her pink robe on the patio with her pink hair curlers in. It was late. I was surprised to see her still awake. One thing about grandma was that she always took perfect care of her appearance. Her hair was dyed jet black and her bright red lips, resembling the pinup era were always painted. I once saw an 8mm video of grandma in the 1940s. She was truly stunning. She had large eyes, an hourglass figure, a pencil dress, black curls, and red full lips. She was such a comfort to me and walking in, caused my breathing to relax.

I remember the entire side of their house was covered in roses and there was a nest of snakes. Every year, the snakes were an issue. Grandma was always out there yanking them and cutting their heads off with scissors. She was hilariously brutal. She grew up on a farm and did hard labor much of her childhood. She was tough and a force to be reckoned with. She had no fear at all inside her when it came to creatures or people. Once, there was a neighborhood boy a few years my senior who teased me on her block. Grandma came after him with a rolling pin and he never bothered me again. I would see her stand up to some of the abusive men mom was with and she was a *fright*. She was a well-endowed woman and her pillow bosom made her hugs warm and soft. She was in many ways, ahead of her time. She got a business degree before women did that kind of thing and she played on an all-boys basketball team back in the 1940s. She was illustrious and had a rebellious nature, which I absolutely *loved*. She would not take crap from anyone.

I crawled into bed with my grandmother under her white floral comforter. She was keen on my anxiety and fear. She rubbed my back and whispered soft words into my ear until I fell asleep. "Don't worry." "We will get your mom help." "You are safe." She always knew how to bring me down from the ledge of terror. Her words had the power to hold me in my darkest nights and even to this day, when I am going through any kind of struggle, I hear her whispering to me in the dark. Without my grandparents, I never would have made it.

The school year was almost over. My grandparents felt it was very important for children to have stability and routine. I loved and craved both. There was never routine at moms. There were never rules. I skipped school, stayed up all night, slept all day, and left my room a mess. It didn't matter if I took a shower or brushed my teeth. For a solid summer once, we had no plumbing in our house. We would go to the river or sneak into a hotel pool to bathe. We used a large bucket inside our bathroom to do our business. At one point, we resorted to using towels to wipe with. Our laundry was never clean, our shower was bug-infested, and we never had adequate food. We had cockroaches and they would fall on top of me whenever I would open the cabinets. I learned to use long sticks to open the cupboards.

It was a dirty house. It smelled of cat urine and filth. The carpet was old, and the ceiling was stained. Often, when she was hospitalized, my grandparents would come in with a large dump truck and hall out all her trash. She would get *very* angry when they would do this.

In addition to her mental illness, she also was a hoarder and had a bad case of being very cheap. When I say cheap, I mean to a ridiculous level. She only permitted us to use one square of toilet paper. She didn't believe in deodorant. Soap was not often found in our house. We would get yelled at for using too much soap when we had it. For toothpaste, we always used baking soda and, in the summer, she believed children didn't need shoes. She would say, "Your feet develop their own shoes." My feet were always getting cut up and blistered in the summer months and other kids could run faster and play harder. I was typically grass bound as the hot cement would burn my feet. Once, I caught my foot in the spoke of the bicycle wheel and it was quite painful. Mom said that people only needed to bathe once every two weeks and she was very against any kind of materialistic qualities developing within me. To her, people who valued material things were the worst kind of evil in society. She felt that true hearts were poor people and that materialistic people were evil. She didn't buy things new. All our clothes, shoes, toys, and furniture were free (given to us by churches, friends, or taken off of curbs).

Mom lived off welfare because her illness impacted her ability to work. We grew up very poor and learned to appreciate everything. Our carpet was found on a curb as was our furniture. Our television was free, and my clothes were taken from the thrift store not far from our house. Once per year, a family member took me shopping and that was the absolute highlight of my life at the time. I treasured that one very nice outfit.

We also had several pets throughout the years. One cat got caught in the hoarding mess and wasn't found until later in the summer season when we noticed a foul smell coming from the garage. He was an all-white cat. He died getting caught and trapped in the garbage. Another cat was hit by a car and our rottweiler was locked in my room most days. He would defecate horribly in my room. Once, during my first ever date, the boy came back to my house to hang out. I was very ambivalent about him seeing my home, however; his father was friends with my step-dad so I assumed we were both from the same type of background and he wouldn't judge me. When we walked into my room, we found around 6 piles of dog feces. That smell stayed in my bedroom until I graduated high school. The smell made it hard to sleep and often I would keep the window open to air out the smell. I associated a dirty house with a messy mind because my mother struggled with being clean. My room was the cleanest part of the home. I would clean it with perfection.

Mom didn't feel that animals needed to be fed, specifically the cats. She felt that they should kill birds, snakes, and mice for food, therefore our pets were skinny and always begging for food. We were taught to eat our meals at various churches or get free food. The cookie store around the corner would always give out the stale cookies to the children, instead of throwing them in the trash. We also found a church around the corner who would give us drinks and snacks. We found a park which provided free lunch and my grandparents were always a source for me, in the event we had nothing.

One summer, mom found that I had lice. She proceeded to put an entire jar of mayonnaise on my hair. It took five months to get the grease out of my hair and the lice were still very much alive in my scalp. She sometimes came up with odd ideas, which would make no sense. Once, she set up a homemade basketball hoop in our backyard. The hoop was made of a wire closet hanger, the backboard was a particleboard. The large pole was a large piece of plywood. It was highly unstable. It was not cemented down and the first basket to go in the hoop, literally caused the entire jerry-rigged pole to come crashing down on the kids in my neighborhood. A really annoying habit she formed was keeping garbage and taking in other people's garbage. She liked dumpster diving, curb shopping, and sometimes stealing from the thrift store a block away. We had *so* much junk. We had a two-legged chair, which she was adamant, was still a viable sitting chair. She had one boot which was very cute that she didn't want to part with. She argued we might run into a paraplegic who needed that one boot. We had bikes with no wheels, broken plates, garbage covered in animal feces, crinkled up papers, and piss-soaked laundry. Everything that came into the home never left.

Life was one ever-changing day of craziness to an even crazier day, with no sense of predictability. I never knew what would happen one day to the next. Because of this, I mentally prepared myself for anything.

During the times when I stayed with my grandparents, their stability was satiating to my soul. I craved stability. I could count on having shampoo, toothpaste, and a warm blanket. Mom sometimes left the thermostat off and we would have to wear coats around our house because she didn't want an expensive electricity bill, so warmth was something I was grateful for. If things were broken or empty, my grandparents would throw them in the trash. In fact, they *had* trash bags. My stomach was full and there was a sense of predictability. We woke every morning, ate a big breakfast, I took a shower every day, and then they would drop me off to school in Des Moines. Their house was impeccable, and their towels were clean. Grandma was a typical 50's housewife. At mom's, I frequently picked soiled, urine-soaked dirty clothes off the basement floor to wear. One day, the shirt was soaked in cat urine, but I was in a hurry and didn't notice. That was a brutal day for me at school and I received a lot of comments. I remember also having mud streaks on my clothes and some of the kids commenting about the dirtiness of my clothing. When I would live with my grandparents, I looked clean and put together.

They always made sure my hair and teeth were brushed and that I had lunch money. After school, I would do homework, eat dinner regularly, practice the piano, and then play. Food was something mom never had much of in her house. I don't necessarily think her not having food was due to her being cheap. I think she had some strong fears regarding food. I believe she thought that by keeping food away, that would cause me to not have weight issues. Thinness mattered to her.

The food not being in our home developed some unhealthy relationships for me with food as an adult. Because I frequently went without food as a child, I would binge eat when I was provided food. I didn't know when I would get to eat again, so I would stuff myself until I was in pain. As a kid, I would turn in bottles and cans and then use that money to purchase junk food from the store a block away. She usually didn't keep track of where I was. I could buy pop for $0.15. I didn't know certain fruits or vegetables. We simply never ate those.

Mom would say, "You only need to eat once a day." She was critical and obsessive about my weight. Being fat to her was the worst thing you could be. There was a lot of emphasis put on beauty and not enough emphasis placed on intelligence, character, kindness, or goodness. A girl's value was based on the type of body she flaunted. A girl's worth was *validated* because of the opinion of a man. That was the message I received from mom frequently.

When I was nine, I would show up to church events where they provided free food. One church would feed the kids entire meals and a nearby park, also provided free lunch. We went there every day. When she would splurge on food (usually the grandparents would bring food to our house), our family would eat and eat, not knowing if in a few days we would have no food. I remember stuffing myself at my grandparent's until I nearly threw up. I would be draped over the chair in horrible pain from overeating. It was fear-based eating. There was a fear that coexisted with food for years to come. I was always afraid I wouldn't get to eat again for a while so I would overeat in fear. There were very unhealthy patterns with food.

When mom was missing, both of my grandparents made it clear that I was under no circumstances to leave with mom. She was considered a danger and their plan was to get her into a mental hospital. In order to get her into a mental hospital, there needed to be two close family members who agreed to admit her and then the police would pick her up. We also had court orders, but it seemed those never truly helped because she wouldn't take her medication regardless. If it was deemed she was a harm to herself or others, and two family members attested, they would admit her into psychiatric care. Once in the behavioral health facility, she was forced to take medication and sleep.

It was *always* a fight and she never went to the hospital willingly. She would never take her medication willingly. It was always a struggle.

CHAPTER 5 - KIDNAPPED

During the time mom wasn't well, I was staying with my grandparents and she and her boyfriend kidnapped me. It began on an early spring day in Iowa. There was still a chill in the air. I sat in my in 3rd-grade class on the 2nd floor, with an empty field to my right as I stared out the window. I was the student who mostly daydreamed. I had a hard time focusing and wasn't truly present in class or in life for that matter. I worried and had things on my mind constantly. Grandma told me that mom was very sick, and I was not to leave with her. They were working on getting her help but couldn't locate where she was.

As I sat in class, I heard a commotion in the hallway. I noticed mom standing at the door. She had an angry stare and demanded I come into the hallway. I knew her well enough to know, she would make a scene, so I left the classroom. At this point, the police had been unsuccessful in locating mom in order to bring her to the mental hospital. The teacher did not know of the sensitive family situation. My grandparents always kept her illness a secret.

As we got into the hallway, she tightened her grip, yanking my arm down the stairwell. She began shouting. "You are the worst child. You're mine, not theirs. You think you can leave me?" She was putting the blame of me being with my grandparents onto me even though they took me because she was having a spell. Being an 8-year-old, her illness scared me. Sometimes I thought it wasn't really *her* being cruel, but it was the *illness* tearing me to pieces but, in my child-mind, I felt confused. She could obliterate my sense of worth and confidence in one sentence. She seemed to have a keen ability to tap into the crack in my soul and blow it wide open. She could sniff fear out, exploit it, and use it to destroy a person. Her words had the power to cut to the marrow. I both loved her unconditionally but also feared her greatly because of her unpredictability.

She demanded I leave with her, threatening, "If you don't come right now, you'll never see me again." I began to cry. "Do you hear me?" "I'll be done with you", she threatened. I begged her to let me call my grandparents and she firmly said, "We are done with them." She took my arm as I reluctantly walked to the car with her, her grip tight against my arm. I didn't want to leave with her. I did it because I feared I would never see her again.

Dane was waiting in the car with a cigarette in his mouth and an annoyed expression smeared across on his face. His swollen face indicated he had been drunk very recently. His skin would be very swollen when he would drink. He looked like he held food inside his cheeks.

Dane had perfected the angry glare, and this was one of his many talents. He loved to shoot ugly stares in my direction. He also liked to flash his penis and ass. He did this, of course, when we were alone. When I would tell mom, she always believed his version of the story, which involved me being a horrible child.

As soon as I got in, he sped off. His car had a sunroof. Rolling all of the windows down, he didn't care that I was freezing. He always had the radio on full blast, usually Alice in Chains or Black Sabbath. There are certain songs, to this day, which take me back to moments in my past. Metallica, Quiet Riot, and Megadeath are a few bands that played the soundtrack of my childhood.

He drove the same way he lived his life, erratically. We drove for what seemed like a long time. I was very cold and felt afraid because I didn't know what was coming next. She hadn't checked me out of school; she simply walked me out the side door. This was before schools were locked and school was still in session. My grandparents didn't know. All I could think about was my grandma's words, "Do not leave with her." I felt the knots in my stomach began to twist. Fast thoughts began darting through my worried mind.

We pulled into an apartment complex. It appeared we were far away from the city of Des Moines. I stretched my eyes but could not find the familiar land markers anywhere around me such as the principal building or Des Moines capital. I later found out he lived in Ankeny. (Many years later, I found that my biological father worked a block away from his apartment complex.) The complex was brown with chipped paint and two levels. The front sidewalk had a large crack where the tree pushed the sidewalk up. There were beer cans on the lawn and the hedges were unkempt.

He was never a kind man; not to me. The memories I have of Dane were of him watching porn openly, flashing body parts, him hurting my mom, and shooting ugly glares in my direction. I remember him beating my mother and sexually assaulting her in front of me. He was the kind of man who enjoyed making you watch him hurt other people. Once, he held a gun to my mother's head and told me he would pull the trigger. He would get something out of breaking me emotionally. There was a sick pleasure on his face from the terror he inflicted. He received some kind of satisfaction from hurting others. He was a very large man in height and weight and for many years to come, I secretly harbored a fear of large men with black curly hair. Years later, there was a man in my church who looked like him. Every time I was around this lookalike, I would feel a panic attack coming on. Any reminder of memories with him tend to be very painful, even to this day.

Dane had a best friend named James who was just as much of a drunk and druggie as he was. He was violent as well. James had a daughter my age name, Mia. Mia had bright red hair and green eyes. I had memories of being at James' house with his daughter Mia, and James coming in to rape her in front of me in the night. James would make us take baths together and watch. One time, James got confused and went to grab for me in the night instead of Mia. He realized what he had done and proceeded to reach for her. It was a frightening experience for me. I closed my eyes, listened to her sobs, and prayed it would end quickly. Mia always had a strong smell from her vagina, which I later found was an attempt to keep her father away. She thought that by not bathing that area, he would stop raping her. When we were about ten, she tried to get me to do sexual things with her and I pushed her off. At the time, I was very angry and disgusted, but I now understand she was a victim of horrible, unimaginable abuses. She was very confused about the impropriety of what her father had done to her.

During my kidnapping in Ankeny, were the loneliest memories in my life. Very early in the morning, Dane would put me outside, like a dog. It was very cold, and the front of the building was completely shaded. Dane would tell me to not leave the square of cement or else I would get beat or be forced to strip naked. He liked to take my clothes off in public places as a form of punishment and humiliation. Once, he told my mother he wanted to take me to the park. I was suspicious of his kind act. While swinging on the swings at a park, he thought that I pushed a girl too hard on the swings, so he forced me to take off my pants and underwear, baring my ass. He then made me stand atop the picnic table and he encouraged the other children to taunt me for, what he convinced the children, was a fat ass. I could tell in their faces, that they were afraid of him like I was. The ways he hurt me broke down every square inch of trust I ever had as a child and it wasn't much. It took me decades to regain a sense of trust after the damage he inflicted. It took me a long time before I could truly trust men, especially tall, curly black-haired men. He traumatized me.

In his moments of torture, I learned to go to another place. I would dream I was sitting by a beach next to someone who loved me. I would dream of going to Hollywood and visiting Disneyland. I would dream of being a singer or an actress; of being friends with Fred Savage, whom I had a crush on at the time. I would dream of *anything* that would allow me an escape for a few moments from the emotional pain he inflicted. I told myself, I'm not here right now.

He had very strict rules for me while I lived in his apartment. I had to sleep on the floor. I wasn't allowed a blanket and under no circumstances was I ever to touch the phone, the fridge, the cabinets, the remote, the television, or his bedroom door. I had to ask permission to use the restroom. He was a very controlling man and he made it abundantly clear that he hated and resented my existence.

At this lonely complex, I would sit on the cracked sidewalk for hours. It was a very lonely time in my life. I was cold. I was hungry. Most of all, I felt afraid. I didn't know where I was, why I wasn't in school, or if I'd ever see my grandparents again. I felt afraid constantly that he would abuse or humiliate me. He was the kind of man that you had to walk on eggshells around, but it also became clear that walking on eggshells didn't help *anyway*. His mood was very unpredictable. He was a tormented person, even when he was around his family.

He wouldn't allow me to have contact with my mom during this time. I felt he was jealous of our relationship and connection and did whatever he could to get rid of me. I felt truly alone. I had a lot of time by myself and that's where I began my tendency to daydream. I would sometimes take a rock and draw on the cement or I would pull up grass, tearing it into small pieces. Sometimes, I would pick apart cigarette butts or pick the gum off the sidewalk. I would clean the cracks or gather sticks or twigs and play like this for hours. Sometimes, I would braid my hair or just watch the ants.

One day, as I sat out in my usual spot on the cracked cement tearing apart cigarette butts, a woman named Mary approached me with a few bags of groceries. She approached me saying, "Honey, what are you doing out here so early? Why aren't you in school? It's way too cold for you to be out here." Sensing my sadness, she put down her groceries and helped me to my feet. "Come inside," she insisted. I told her he watched me and pointed up toward the window. "If I leave the cement square, it will spell trouble for me." She said, "Nonsense. I won't let him hurt you." She promised, and I believed her.

When I walked into Mary's apartment, she immediately began cooking me a meal. She was a gentle, kindhearted woman with compassion in her heart for me. As I write this, I feel the tears behind my eyes because she will never know how much her act of kindness meant to me. Mary saw me. She noticed me. She pulled me up, wrapped a blanket around me, and made me a meal. I was a child in deep pain and her act of kindness meant more to me than anything at the time. It was the first touch and first expression of love I felt in what seemed like ages. My soul was thirsty, and she nourished it. We sat on her couch and she turned on her television, putting on cartoons. She said she had children, but they were older. She had plants all around her apartment and I noticed his apartment seemed dark and empty. Her apartment was surrounded in sunlight and it seemed welcoming, warm, and inviting, just like she seemed warm and inviting.

It wasn't long, that I began to hear his screams in the hallway for me. I could hear his fists pounding the walls and doors. "Where are you, bitch?", he ranted. He had a booming voice that instantly caused a fear. Just the sound of his voice, caused panic to arise in me. It felt like a knife ripping into my stomach. My face became hot. My body started to shake. I began the familiar labored breathing, heart-pounding, and dry mouth experience. The panic began to come in waves, taunting that the "death feeling" would now come at any moment. When you have a panic attack, it literally feels like you are dying.

At that, Mary went into the hallway and said, "How dare you. What is wrong with you?" He pushed his way through the door to find me sitting on the couch wrapped in a blanket. His face looked murderous and my fear was *so* big that I wasn't even sure this was really happening. It felt like a movie was playing. I was watching it, not living it. My body felt numb and noises seemed to slur, and everything slowed down. I had a physical reaction to the fear I felt in my chest.

He dragged me back to his apartment where he began pushing me in front of my mother saying, "Do you know what this bitch did?" I was crying. It angered me that she allowed him to hurt me like that. She believed every lie from his disgusting lips. She just stood there and let him hit me. She gave weak responses and slight agreements. She provided no protection at all from his rage. I had anger in me toward her for being so weak. I hated her weakness and thought to myself, I will never be vulnerable like you. She had no ability to rise against him and no strength at all in herself. He had her completely under his control with the fear.

He continued to push me, threatening and demanding I take my clothes off. "Take them off!", he screamed. I began to shake. I could barely stand. "No," I sobbed and pleaded. "I'll rip them off." At this point, I began shaking. He took the clothes off me and forced me outside. He said, "You will stand with your ass in traffic until you learn." He made dramatic hand gestures for people to look at me and my naked ass. At that moment, I was completely shattered and broken. I felt so hurt and alone. I could hear Mary's stomps and shouts. The next thing I know, she grabbed me and ushered me back into the building. I honestly blacked out much of the next memory but from what I can recall, there was a physical altercation. There were spotted images of what felt like him trying to kill my mother, and of Mary taking punches at our expense.

It's all fragmented pieces. I remember him dragging me into his bedroom and the phone crashing against the wall. I remember seeing a gun in his hand. The next thing I remember was an African American police officer picking me up, into her arms. "You are okay now," she told me. "I have you." I was still sobbing as she held me. She wrapped a blanket around me as she walked back to her police car.

There are a few incidents, which are completely blacked out for me with Dane. One involved him and his best friend James forcing me into the basement and taking my pants off. I see stacks of porn magazines on the floor and feel him accusing me of looking at his porn. Mom had just left us alone with him. I see images of Mia completely naked. I literally do not remember what happened because it is all black but get a sick feeling when I think of it or that basement.

CHAPTER 6 – MENTAL HOSPITAL

I was never so happy in my life to see my grandparents. My grandpa picked me up and held me in his arms. He always tried to take a person from a dark place to a bright place. He took me back to their house. I was so relieved to be out of that hell. *Finally*, mom was being forced into the mental hospital. I don't have a clear timeline of how long I lived in that apartment in Ankeny, but to *me*, it felt like ages.

Receiving help is what was best for *her* and all of us. Now, finally, this affliction upon our family would hopefully end.

Dane was put back in jail. He ended up going to prison. He hated and blamed mom for his incarceration. He has never taken responsibility for his actions. He never saw anything wrong with his violence or behavior.

There was nothing that could be done to get him out of the trouble he created. At the knowledge of him being gone, I breathed deeper. I slept better. A sense of calm washed over me like never before. I could breathe again.

Some years later, I heard a rumor that after he got out of prison, he went back into prison. The second time, he was in for charges involving raping a child. This didn't surprise me, not in the least. As for his best friend James, he *also* went to prison for rape and was later murdered.

It was several days before they allowed mom to have visitors in the mental hospital. I got back in school and my grandparent's routine picked up. Usually, it would take a while for mom's brain to get reset and for her to be put back on track. I believe this was because she had so much stubborn resistance. She never took her medication and resented the mental hospital and everyone in it. She hated the family during this time. We were all evil assholes in her mind. Every time she was put in the mental hospital, pieces of her disappeared. She came out an angrier version. It chipped and whittled at the kind mother I once knew. The trusting and kind part of her began to die and this cruel, mean, and vindictive person began to surface. It seemed that darkness was being poured in and the light was leaving.

Certain people within our family grew very tired of the drama that came from mental illness. She burned every bridge. She pissed people off. Most people in the family to this day, refuse to talk to her. I find this sad because although I understand, the illness is not her. I think of mental illness like any other disease such as cancer, diabetes, or aids. Having cancer doesn't make a person *be* cancer. What I mean is mental illness is not the person, it's the disease. I see the two as separate. I know my sweet and loving mother is locked in there somewhere underneath it all. I was always convinced, we have to find her and bring her out.

When she would be in a spell she would not eat for days, stay up all night, have paranoia, and talk to herself. She would go into grand delusions and hear things. Once, I woke to her standing over my bed. She had a crinkled-up piece of paper in her hand, which she was crinkling in both hands over me, while I slept. She looked like the person from the movie, The Ring. Hair hung in her face, her eyes were wide, and she scared the life out of me. I immediately shot up out of sleep and jumped out of the bed so fast at the sight of her. She ran off and suddenly a thousand noises were filling the atmosphere, all at once. I went into the living room and found the television volume had been turned on full blast. The radio volume was turned on full blast. A running vacuum sat in an upright position, in the middle of the living room, running. A million sounds all at once were screaming and if I wasn't already awake, the shock of that noise jolted me awake.

I found her standing in the kitchen with a hammer in her right hand, nails, and a pinecone in her left hand. She stood at the sink with her back facing me. She was ferociously beating the nails into a pinecone and her hands were bloody. She was mumbling to herself. "Mom, what are you doing?", I asked. She didn't answer and continued driving the nails into the pinecone until the entire pinecone was surrounded in nails and there were small red remnants on the pinecone from where her blood had soaked in.

I hesitated but decided to turn down all the glaring sounds that were drowning us out from the living room. I heard a noise in the back bedroom. There, I found a relative still asleep, miraculously, amidst all the noise. I noticed they were surrounded in a dozen light bulbs encircling them and there was a mallet placed next to their head. It was very odd. She followed me into the room saying, "I'm protecting them from evil, see?", pointing to the light bulbs. She still had the pinecone in her hand, and I asked her again, "What are you doing with that?" "I'm making a present for grandpa. Isn't it nice?" She chatted to herself and her words made no sense at all. She spoke frantically, pulverizing the pinecone with ferocious whispers. Interactions such as these were normal, and I got used to seeing my mother fall apart. But seeing her like this was never easy.

I was her caretaker, her mother and expected to put her back together again, or at least attempt to. I was the fixer, and it was my role in the family from a young age to be responsible for her wellbeing. If she fell apart, then I wasn't working hard enough. My family made sure that I understood that it was *my* job to make sure that she was okay. The only problem with that was that I was never allowed to be a child. I have very few memories where I remember playing and laughing. You sometimes see children get lost in fun and I was never really able to do this without those constant companions: worry, fear, and shame. I was a parent to my parent. There was always high alert, worry, anxiety, and concern locked within my brain. Worrying about her was a full-time job and I had to mentally prepare myself for any and everything *all* the time. I would map out possibilities in my head every night because then I wouldn't be so surprised at the next impending disaster. I never felt she was okay to be left alone and I was her babysitter of sorts. By readying myself for the catastrophe that was my life, it somehow gave me a sense of preparedness. I suppose it gave me a false sense of control.

Her delusions were confusing to me as a child. Once, she was convinced two men broke into her home. She went on to tell me they broke every window, ripped her carpet, broke her door, and tore out her electrical wiring. I immediately called someone to assess the situation. Upon review, all the lights worked, no windows were broken, the door was locked, and the carpet was untorn. As a child, sometimes her beliefs and behavior would be very confusing for me. Was it real, or not real? Am I wrong, or she wrong? Thus, confusion became a prevalent factor in the realm of my mind.

Once my mother was convinced that she was on the news and the cops were pursuing her. She felt the police were after me and my sister also. I could feel her increased paranoia and anxiety. She was so convincing that I thought maybe this *was* real. I frantically began combing the news stations and calling everyone I knew to see if mom was, in fact, on the news. I found out quickly that this was a delusion in her mind. To her, it was real, but in real life it was not happening.

One time I saw her come undone at a restaurant. When the waitress brought her plate over, she began screaming, violently swinging, and throwing her plate. She was having a delusion that there were hundreds of bugs on her dinner plate. The waitress stared at us with serious and sincere concern. She saw no bugs. I saw no bugs. However, mom was coming undone. I could see the confusion and fear on the waitress's face. It was outbursts such as these that made me fear my emotions greatly. I thought that if I felt an emotion, I might be crazy like my mother.

Once she was doing home repair while naked and a relative came over. He observed her odd and unconventional behavior, cleaning the house in the nude.

They got into an altercation and he told her to put some clothes on. She argued, "You have a problem with nudity. That is your issue, not mine." She went on to hang curtains in the nude.

Moments such as these were normal, and I had to be able to overlook a lot because of her condition.

The first time we visited her at the mental hospital, there was a large, thick metal door entering the ward. I remember there were about six people standing by the door as we entered. There was a musty smell. The smell reminded me of an elderly home. One woman had gray hair and yellow teeth. She got very close to my face asking repeatedly, "Have you seen her?" She asked me this question probably twenty times. I felt very uncomfortable with her lack of distance. A man called out to me thinking I was his child. He was excited his daughter came to visit. We waited in the main hall for mom to come out of her room, while several of the mental patients wondered and circled like zombies around the door. Another asked grandpa for a cigarette where he oddly emphasized the word ci-gar-ette. There were people clapping, screaming, and one lady sounded as if she was dying. She was screaming, "Help!" It was a blood-curdling cry, and the staff simply ignored it. In fact, one of the staff members, a middle-aged African American woman, was singing a happy jingle. I couldn't understand how she could try to act normal in this crazy place. It set me on edge. The furniture was blue and had a lot of padding. Being in this place was a very frightening experience for me as an eight-year-old.

Finally, someone brought mom out. Her hair was matted against her face and her eyes kept staring into a blank abyss. She wore a hospital gown and it looked as if she were somewhere else entirely from a mental standpoint. The paranoid, panicked, fighting mother I knew a week ago turned into a numbed-out zombie. Her face was emotionless and unreadable. When she would get like this,

I often worried she would never come back to us. I didn't know where she retreated to inside herself, but I hoped she would find her way out and back to her family.

"Mom," I said. I tapped her. She just kept staring into space with her greasy hair stuck against her cheek; her eyes completely glazed over.

In this room, there was a tan exercise bike; the kind with a built-in fan. My grandpa encouraged me to ride the bike and blow some air toward him, while he and grandma talked with mom. Grandpa always had a way of breaking through with mom that none of us had. Much later in life, after he died, I was terrified we would have to permanently put her away because he was the *only* one who could bring her back out of the dark place within herself. They had a special connection which I'll never understand. The relationship between mom and grandma was highly strained, however, which I also never understood. To me, grandma was amazing and years later mom would tell me how hard it was to have a daughter that looked and acted just like her mother, whom she hated. Apparently, grandma and I are very similar.

It was a short visit and every time we would come back to see her; a very small piece of mom would just barely reveal itself. I would notice a small smile, a tone, or that she brushed her hair. I noticed her talking made more sense and she seemed clearer in her head. I had many moments where I wondered if she would be gone forever. I had many moments where I didn't think she would ever be truly okay inside, but slowly she always came back to us. For that, I was grateful.

CHAPTER 7 – DRUG AND PARTY HOUSE

Mom stayed in the mental hospital for what seemed like a long time. She got out in July of 1989. She had met two friends while in the mental hospital, and they were going to come over and stay at our house for a while. Mom always had a desire to take in homeless people and to help them in their life. This opened us to some really dangerous situations, but she was certain that these people needed her help. Ironically, she couldn't help herself (or me), but she loved helping the homeless.

Becky, from the mental hospital, looked a lot like mom. She had brown hair and the same build. Mom said that she had bipolar disorder. The guy with Becky was creepy. He wore a large cowboy hat with tight green biker shorts and brown cowboy boots. His fashion and personality seemed very off and mismatched. He had black curly hair, which was my mom's type. Eventually, this odd man would grow comfortable enough to prance around our living room and sprawl out on our Papasan chair in a leopard bikini. For obvious reasons, I found him very inappropriate and disturbing.

They moved into our home and every night there would be wild parties into the early hours of the morning. It became difficult to focus and I struggled a lot because of the lack of sleep. Later in the fall, when school was in session, the teachers thought I had a learning disability. But it was later discovered that my home life contributed to my school struggles. Department of Human Services would get involved and my grandparents would talk to me beforehand, prepping me on what to say to DHS, in order to circumnavigate me being taken from mom. This was when my lying became very normal; the line between the truth and the version I was telling created confusion. I was questioned many times over the years by counselors and authorities and much of what I told them was based upon what my grandparents told me to tell them.

The parties got bigger as did the group of people who began to live in our house.

Around this time, there was a house three doors down on the same block, which was later featured on the six-o-clock news. This house had the largest drug bust in the history of Iowa, and a man was also killed nearby. He had been gunned down on the sidewalk and to this day, they have never been able to solve the case. Just like our house, their house had wild parties every single night of the week. The people from their house began coming to ours and that's how mom met Joe.

It became normal having dozens of strangers in our home. Things like porn on the television, sex on the couch, needles, cocaine, pot, and alcohol were all frequent fun events at these parties. There would be dancing and sometimes fighting. We had an old guy named Wiseman who was the hippie philosopher of the group, a man named Bones who was the bleached-out muscle guy of the group, T-Bone was the quiet one, and Johnny Boy was the guy who supplied the drugs. There was Jason who was known for his robbery and conman skills, Annie who was quiet, Chris who slept with nearly every girl he came in contact with, Amy who was a girl version of Chris, Scooby who had a love of weed, Coop who was the most handsome and popular of the group, and several others. There was an older lady named Bonnie who had some gray and blonde in her hair and liked to wear very revealing outfits in which her breasts were spilled out. Her common attire involved a tight leather mini-skirt with a shirt that resembled a bra. Bonnie had a son named Ben who had large brown eyes and big 80's hair. I had a small crush on Ben who was just a year older than me. Ben was sensitive and his older brother was a bad boy who ran around the neighborhood stealing things. Ben's older brother, PJ, was known for being in a gang. Bonnie was a severe alcoholic and when she would come over, she was incredibly cruel and mean. Bonnie started sleeping with her older son's friend (her eldest son was seventeen), and Bonnie was deeply insecure about every beautiful girl she crossed paths with. In that way, her hatred of me was not personal in the slightest but self-doubt within her.

She was an angry drunk and loved to cut me down with her words until I would disappear. I was a beautiful young girl who developed breasts by the time I was ten. I looked much older than I really was. She would get a look of satisfaction when I genuflected. She was presumably happy that she won when she would force me to leave. Mom seemed to thank her as if when I was gone, they could really have fun. I was happy to leave, not to mention Bonnie's boyfriend Bill was incredibly homely. He was a meth user. His eyes were always dilated, his hair was frizzy and bleached white, and his skin had large divots.

She especially liked to be cruel to me in front of her son Ben. One time, I went to her duplex. It was a one-bedroom down the road. Roaches covered the walls of the small room. I was shocked at the number of roaches in their home because our house also had bugs, however, their house was literally covered wall to ceiling infested with bugs. There were maggots in the trashcan, which overflowed outside the duplex. It smelled very badly of feces, they had fleas, and her son Ben was sitting on the bed in his white underwear playing Nintendo. I awkwardly sat next to him watching him play, while his mom got high.

The smell of weed filled the one-room duplex. "Look at that fucking slut," she drunkenly slurred. Part of me felt like this boy and I had an unspoken connection, perhaps, because of the similar homelife situation, we both endured. He was shy as was I. We didn't talk much but when our parents would get high together, we would play video games together on his stained mattress. Usually, I would watch him play. He seemed to be unaware that he was only wearing underwear and that there were a dozen or so people crammed into his small one-bedroom duplex.

I later discovered during an alcohol run that Bonnie's van was a stolen vehicle. Most likely her eldest son PJ stole it for her. The seats were milk crates and the spot for the ignition was completely exposed wire. Two wires would need to be touched in order to get the van running and the VIN number had been scratched out. I remember the van was very dirty and smelled like alcohol, and I found it odd that Bonnie demanded we wear seatbelts as we sat on milk crates, while she drove whilst intoxicated.

Every night was the same. Everyone would drink, get high, crank the music, dance, and grind, get naked and party all night. Fights would break out, usually over women flirting with someone's man, or someone owing another person money, or someone not loaning a cigarette to another person. It was all petty. The crowd moved from the duplex at Ben's, to our place, and three doors down to the drug house. For a time, our house was the most popular party house on the block.

During this time, I took my hiding tendency to a new level and found ways to not be home. All the noise made it difficult. No one really noticed my escapism or noticed me for that matter. They were preoccupied with sex, drugs, parties, fighting, and generally being loud.

I didn't like the noise, the parties, the constant fights and the police showing up at our house. I would find myself for hours thinking of ways in which I could leave this house. I started reaching my limit and had enough of all the lawless chaos that encircled my life.

CHAPTER 8 - JOE

At one of these block parties, in the summer of

1989, mom met Joe. Joe looked a lot like Slash from Guns

N' Roses. He had jet black curly hair, with big eyes, and a

babyface. He wore a leather hat and he was covered in

devil tattoos. On his chest, he had a large devil tongue

licking the crotch of a woman and he also had several

women's names tattooed on his arm along with naked

breasts. Each name would be crossed out and a new name

added underneath. I think there were five or so names during the time I knew him.

Joe was a lot younger than mom. The first night they met, they had loud annoying sex. I know because I heard every single disgusting detail. They were never coy about their rendezvous. It was common to find used condoms, needles, beer bottles, and remnants of cocaine. I actually didn't mind Joe in comparison to Dane, who recently exited our life, due to his jail-bird status. Joe just seemed to want to have fun all the time. He was a high school dropout, a drug lover, a sex lover, a thief, and a conman. He was magnetic and a clown who would get very clumsy when loaded, and often became the center of howling laughs when he would nosedive into the carpet. He was most certainly, the life of the party and everyone loved him. His main game at getting what he wanted was using his charm. He was very popular with the ladies and quite manipulative at getting what he wanted from them.

One night, the main drug dealer in our part of town came to our house. It was a big deal because Joe had an opportunity to work for him and make some money under the table. None of the guys Joe ran with ever worked nine to five jobs. They all hustled and did things like steal, work under the table, hustle, or deal drugs. Joe himself rarely worked, but when he did it was always jobs which were done off the books, mostly schemes he would come up with to earn a quick dollar.

He was known to rob liquor stores, gas stations, people's homes, and local businesses. Stealing things and conning people was his main source of income. He was such a charmer. But drug dealing would be more lucrative.

I remember Gage coming into our home. There were fifty or so people and the place was packed. Smoke filled the air and the music was booming. There were people out front, in the backyard, and filled every room of our small smoke infested house. The dealer had a small entourage that followed him around. Music was pumping and as he walked in, people cleared a path for him. I noticed that he walked in with a cane and dressed in a lot of gold, with much of it on his fingers. He had some metal in his teeth and had several tattoos around his face and the back of his neck was shaved. He seemed to be of Hispanic origin. I also remember his car was a 1984 Monte Carlo decked out in bright rims, low tires, black tint, and you could hear the thump of the stereo a mile away.

Gage and Joe sat at the kitchen table and Gage laid out a cocktail of drugs. I got the feeling that Joe felt like the popular kid was talking to him. I watched as Joe's eyes grew in size at the sight of these drugs laid out on our kitchen table. Mom told me to go to my room. At that, I left and I'm not sure what went down but can only assume they got high.

It was common to find people having sex in my room. That was another thing that really annoyed me. Once, I walked in on a couple having sex on my floor. He was on top of her, thrusting inside of her. She was a married friend of my mothers and I remember being surprised at finding them because she had just had her first baby with her husband. Her husband was nice and hard working. I asked them to leave and he tried to pay me off so he could finish screwing her. It was disgusting. There was another time I found a friend of Joe's in my room. He had a purple French tickler condom in his hand with a grin spread across his cheeks as if he were waiting for me. I knew he wanted to sleep with me. He was very obvious, and frankly, I knew other girls in my neighborhood who were having sex at ages eleven and twelve. He asked me, "Want to see how a French tickler works?" He pulled it out and dangled it in front of me. I responded, "No, not really." He proceeded to pull me onto his lap. I could smell the liquor on his breath and watched his eyes roll in his head as he began to whisper and slur sexual words to me. I stood up and asked him to leave but he went on to explain that the tickler tickles a girl's pussy and feels really good. My face flushed at his use of the word pussy. I felt ashamed, embarrassed, annoyed, and out of my depth at this creepy man in my room. I will admit that he was a cute older man but at least fifteen years my senior and this was gross and inappropriate. Joe came looking for him and they went off. I was relieved to be rid of this man.

Another time, there was a man who was eighteen and I was age eleven. He grabbed my crotch and began stroking it on the dancefloor. I wore a thin jean dress and he had full access to my groin. The music was playing, and I happened to cross the dance floor, when he grabbed me forcefully and started feeling me up, grinding against me. The song playing on the radio was "I Wanna Sex you Up," I struggled to get loose from his grip. I nearly had a panic attack as I ran out of the house. I ran out into the cold night and sat by the swings. When I later told people about it, the next day, they gave an excuse saying, "Oh he was drunk. He didn't know." The same thing was said of the purple French tickler guy. I knew better because twice I found him waiting until mom and Joe left the house. Then, when I was alone, he tried to convince me to open the door for him saying he wanted to talk. There was a pattern of sexual predation. One of my relatives lost her virginity at a party at the age of fourteen to an older man who seduced her just like this guy tried to pursue me.

I recall another time, where a man in his 30's frequently loitered around our house. One time, I was in the backyard, laying out in a bikini. Everyone was gone. This strange man came into my yard and sat next to me on the ground. I jumped out of my skin when I noticed him. I was so incredibly uncomfortable when he began speaking about how his wife slept with a teacher when she was fourteen and that dating an older man was a good experience. I thought I might be raped. I was afraid. I managed to run in the house and lock the door. He stood at the door, asking me to open it. I tried to tell this information, but my parents would blame *me,* my attire, or say it was made up in my head. They claim I somehow misconstrued. I learned early that my feelings were wrong and as a result questioned my deductive reasoning for years. The truth was much more painful. They didn't care that I was being hurt. They were too cowardly to deal with it. They allowed it. There was no justice or recourse.

I never felt safe sexually, emotionally, mentally, or physically in this house. It was all a game in my mind of how long I could possibly endure living in hell. Most nights, I survived hiding in my room, hiding in my books, staying in my closet, or hiding outside.

CHAPTER 9 – THE TURF WAR

During one of those countless nights of parties, a fight broke out at our house. There was an accusation from the ringleader of the drug house three doors down, that some valuable (stolen) electronics went missing. There was a bantering back and forth. "We know it was you, pussy," said Tommy. At that, the crowd moved outside onto the street. The focus had been on the men fighting and suddenly to the left, mom and another woman began swinging at one another. This other woman had bleached frizzy crimped hair and was wearing a shirt that showcased her flat stomach. She had a raspy voice as though she had smoked since childhood and wore a short fringe jean skirt. Everyone followed the two women and watched them as they rolled on the white gravel, pulling at each other's hair, hitting, and biting one another. They were shouting, "I'll fuck you up bitch." This was my mom on the ground fighting in front of me. I was around ten years old. It was jarring. I couldn't believe what I was seeing in front of me.

Just then, Joe and the chick's boyfriend, Sean, started throwing fists because one of them was trash-talking the other woman. "She's kicking that bitches' ass!", Joe proudly stated. "That bitch is my old lady," Sean yelled. I watched as the man, who was easily twice the size of Joe, threw Joe into the air like a football. Joe's face landed on the side of the curb with a large thud. Joe didn't even get a hit in before he was knocked out cold. Blood immediately began to pour out as Joe was knocked out and I watched the blood gather on the street. Sean was hubris. He began pounding his chest like a gorilla, throwing slurs in Joe's direction, calling him a pussy and a little bitch. Joe was immediately laid out and not moving at all. The crowd cheered as they watched Sean pound his chest in triumph. People were laughing as if this was a boxing match. I didn't know if Joe would wake from that devastating hit. The crack noise was loud.

Joe stood up a bit dazed and had blood dripping from his head. He stumbled. He was confused and thought that he had won the fight, but his friends taunted him calling him, "Little Punk, who went down like a fucking sack of potatoes." Mom told the woman, "Get the fuck out of here and never come back." At that, the crowd left while Joe stood in the street in a daze and mom's hair had been disheveled and her shirt was ripped open, so her bra was showing. (It was later discovered that Joe, in fact, did steal these electronics and sold them. One of the stereos he gave to me to use in my bedroom along with the tape still in the stereo which was Quiet Riot).

After that, we still had parties at our house but not as large. The people in the drug house three doors down no longer wanted to hang at our place. There was an active turf war going between our two houses over Joe's theft. One of their sons frequently hocked loogies on me at school. He would find slugs to throw on me. I often came home with snot in my hair. He would literally stand there for several seconds snorting, clearing his throat, hocking, in my direction at our bus stop. Many years later, their elder son who was a very angry boy, went to prison for attempted murder and committed suicide. I remember in school, he would walk out of class all the time. None of the teachers could do anything about it. He was out of control. By the eighth grade, he was selling drugs. His death and suicide were a shock to many people.

After that, I felt uncomfortable playing outside and there was always a fear that one of the people from their drug house would jump us, so we tried to remain always in a crowd.

Sometimes I could manage to find a somewhat quiet place in the house.

I began to pursue escapism by reading books during this time. Reading helped me tremendously through the tumultuousness and provided a means of escape. I enjoyed the simplicity of the *Little House on the Prairie* books. I longed to live in a simpler time.

CHAPTER 10 – ROBBERIES, SCAMS, AND CONS

One night, Bones showed up with Wiseman. Bones was overly tan, and a stout, muscular man. He was very stocky and had long, bleached, nearly white hair. He reminded me of a less muscular version of Hulk Hogan in both his look and his attitude. He loved to talk trash. I thought of him as unintelligent. The reason was that these three stooges were constantly trying to come up with a new scam or idea on how to do some form of criminal activity. Frankly, their ideas were utterly stupid. Wiseman was very old and had long gray hair with a long gray beard. He was a local homeless guy who slept behind the gas station and occasionally the grocery store a block away from our home. He was a Gandalf of sorts and spouted quotes and advice to anyone who would listen. He had an old-school hippie vibe and had some similarity to Tommy Chong from the popular "Cheech and Chong," except that his hair reached his butt. He got the name Wiseman because he was philosophical. He would occasionally crash on our couch. Toward the end of Joe and Wiseman's relationship, things ended very badly. This occurred months later. Wiseman owed Joe a pack of cigarettes and couldn't afford to pay. Joe held him down on our front lawn, cut his hair and beard, and burned his hair on our front porch. Smelling the burned hair and seeing Wiseman's red face and tear-filled eyes is something I will never forget.

Another one of Joe's friends Jason was known for being one of the more professional conmen and would join in the conversation as well as Scooby who was usually content to sit in a weed cloud most days. Scooby had five kids with four different women and had a chill and carefree attitude most days.

The men who would commit the crimes together were usually Jason, Joe, and Bones but the other men would offer suggestions.

This day, Bones showed up at our door with pantyhose on his face. He looked absolutely ridiculous. He was amped up on crack cocaine and told Joe that he wanted to rob the gas station two blocks away. As a kid, I became very good at being able to tell when someone was high. With dope, you notice the dilated eyes, leg twitching, the shifty eyes, the tapping hands and inability to sit still. Long-term use unveils bad and dented skin, paranoia, and bad teeth. Mostly, they are skinny, aggressive, and can't sit still. With weed, the eyes get really bloodshot, plus you can smell it a mile away. Weed tends to make people be very calm. Vicodin and Oxy make people get slurry and lethargic. When Joe would be on Oxy, his eyelids were half shut. LSD just makes people insane. Most of the crowd that Joe hung with liked to smoke dope except for Scooby who loved pot.

I could tell that Bones was definitely on cocaine. He was trying to amp Joe up, talking him into robbing this gas station. This particular gas station on the east side of Des Moines had been robbed so many times that they closed it down for good a few years later. They were getting so much money taken, it eventually drove them out of business.

That night, I watched these three stooges raid my mother's pantyhose drawer, put the pantyhose over their faces, and cockily head up to the gas station with bats and two by fours in hand. They looked ridiculous. Because this place caught onto the very recurrent robberies, they only kept a small amount of cash and made frequent trips to the bank. I don't know if these fools used a gun, but I assume they didn't because weapons were expensive, especially for people of our caliber. The men only walked away with a little over $150.00, after the robbery, which according to them was a score. Apparently, when they did this before, they only scored around $100.00.

Not getting enough of a thrill from their gas station robbery adventure, the men talked about where else they could get quick cash. Most nights went on like this. They would all sit in a circle, talking about their incredibly dumb ideas on how to thieve or con money. They would talk about places or people whom they could steal from. "There's this plant off of Army Post, they have a shit ton of copper wire," one of them said. They could sell the copper for around $2-3 a pound. It seemed to me, that the heists they did were more exerted effort than working an actual job. The three stooges set off to steal the copper wire. It was insanely heavy and ended up sitting in our back yard until one of the many times that mom got put back in the mental hospital, and my uncle brought a dump truck to rid her of her junk.

I remember another night; the men were trying to come up with a concoction to make more money. As they sat around a table in a cloud of smoke, I listened to their conversation. It was painful because of the idiocy of some of their incredibly stupid ideas. It seemed between the three of them, there was not one brain cell at work. One had an idea to rob a thrift store just a block down the road. I thought to myself, that's like someone trying to rob the Dollar Tree (really dumb idea in my mind) I would watch as they would counterfeit money. They would take four $100 bills with a $1 bill and rip one corner off each of the four, then tape them onto the $1-dollar bill edges. This scam actually worked for them several times until the newer money began to circulate and electronics caught onto the criminal's schemes. Sometimes the men would rob houses, and it would usually be people they knew. A few of them would tag team and there would always be a distractor and the thief. One of the men would keep the victim's attention while the other would ask to use the bathroom. They would steal jewelry, movies, and typically small items. For larger steals, they would wait until the person left.

Another very frequent scam was to accuse a restaurant of having hair in their food. I would watch them actually clip their hair, place it in the food and then scream out to the hostess. Jason could be quiet convincing, however, one day many years later, I worked in the food industry and saw him doing this scam to my boss. He looked at me with fear on his face, like he had been caught.

The food gimmick was another trick that worked quite often. There was one time, however, when the restaurant would not budge on allowing a free meal. I guess the hostess was up for a fight and would not bend. All of us sat at the table. Joe leaned his head forward saying, "Listen...... Everyone run." At that, we all took off running in different directions. There were maybe seven of us and mom had to drive around the block six times to find everyone in the pitch-black night. The restaurant backed up to a forest. I ended up in some field near a forest. I learned pretty early to not go out to dinner with my family because it usually involved criminal activity. Matter of fact, the very first meal mom took my future husband to was one of these memorable moments. To do this day, (23 years later) he will not go out to dinner with her.

I should also mention that the few friends who did come to my house, usually only visited *once*. I can think of a handful of friends who were no longer allowed to speak with me after coming over. One of those incidences involved a friend Tara. We were told to not leave my bedroom, but we became very thirsty. We also had to use the restroom after several hours. I considered climbing out my window, pissing in my yard, and using the hose to drink from but it was freezing outside so we opted for the bathroom. When we finally walked out of the bedroom, and we stopped at the sight of three naked people on our living room floor having sex. Needless to say, Tara never came over again. Also, she wasn't allowed to talk to me at school and wouldn't return my calls.

The idiotic conversation to scam, rob, or steal, was still going. One of the men's brothers had a brand-new litter of puppies. These puppies were a Rottweiler mix. The plan was that they could sell one of the puppies under the guise of it being a "full" Rottweiler. It was rare for a Rottweiler to have a short tail, however for those who did – the price was higher. This was according to the 3 stooges, anyway.

The problem was that all of the puppies had long tails. The idea suggested, was to chop the tail off of the dog, then scam someone into believing that the dog was a full Rottweiler breed, and then sell the dog at a higher price than it was actually valued at. Again, a lot of work to go through, for a small payoff. This was one of those truly disgusting moments that is painful. One of the idiots left to bring the dog back to our house.

He got back and the dog was very cute and had the little whimper that puppies still have when they are separated from their mother too soon. I begged and pleaded with Joe to not do this. "Can we just keep the dog for our family?", I suggested. I tried to recruit mom into talking him out of this horrible idea. "Mom, do something!" She was weak and said nothing. He would not listen as he was determined to make money off of this poor, innocent animal.

What happened next haunts me. The three men took the small puppy into the basement. I was still pleading with them as they pushed past me down the stairs carrying the crying dog. It became apparent that I was not going to persuade them. I couldn't bear to watch this, so I left the room. Their idea was to hit the tail of the dog with a bat, as to numb the tail, and then proceed to cut the tail off with a jagged knife. I will never, for as long as I live, forget the screams that came from that dog. It was one of the cruelest things I ever heard in my life. Their evil had no bounds, and at that moment, I decided I truly hated Joe. I would never forget this, I decided.

It took several chops and slices to get the tail removed and there was blood everywhere. The dog cried for days. The crying got so bad that they left the puppy outside to avoid hearing the cries. The tail was not cut short enough for the dog to actually pass as a full breed, so when they tried to pull their scam, people knew it was an obvious lie. People caught on quickly. The dog ended up being sold at a cheap price to a friend. I was later told the dog was one of the angriest and most vicious dogs in the neighborhood. It would routinely attack people and I always knew the secret of why that dog was so angry.

One of the lighter scam stories involved a piece of crap car in our yard. A storm from a tornado had ripped through our yard and a very large and old tree had fallen on top of the car. This car was given to us freely by Joe's father. It was an older brown Lincoln Continental covered in rust. Prior to the tree falling on the car, it already had some issues going on. While driving, the car would stall. You would hear a screeching gunshot sound. It would bang in the middle of a drive and then the car would stall for 20 minutes. The car would start again, but the loud bang would occur again, and so forth. This process would repeat so we never drove the car too far away from our home for fear, we would be permanently stuck. We always made sure we were within walking distance.

The tree had fallen on the car. After the tornado-tree-tragedy-incident on the car, looking straight at the car, there was a perfect upside-down triangle on the roof and the car was already quite flat. The triangle point dipped so low that it was impossible to get inside of the car. Bottom line, the car's lifespan was over.

However, Joe and mom were convinced this car was still a mint and still sellable. Never mind, that it had a tree on top of it – they thought it would go for $500.00. I found myself laughing at this notion. What was purely comical about this entire thing was watching the people come to see and test drive the triangle-shaped car. Their first look at the sight of the car, caused numerous buyers to laugh out loud. Some would hold a hand up and walk away with an obvious disgusted expression. But for a very select few, some stubbornly tried to pry their way inside the badly dented car. No one was able to wedge their body inside the car and additionally, the door was very difficult to open. In smashing the car down, it bent the door frame. Long story short, it ended up being scrapped and no one would buy it.

Another comical story involved Joe's quick stint and desire to start a career as a non-licensed Electrician, which was also illegal. He worked for a man for a brief period, who literally looked like the Unabomber. The man had a huge mushroom hairdo with a psychotic expression that was his normal face. This guy set up our doorbell system in our home. Every time people would ring our doorbell, they would get zapped really powerfully. This worked well for Mormons and solicitors, however, for friends we would have to warn them to never touch the metal part of the door. This was especially crucial when it was raining outside. I would tell people, it is best to use the backdoor. Matter of fact, I would rather crawl in the window than use that front door. Joe wanted to go into business with the Unabomber looking guy, doing under the table electrical work.

One day, mom and I were sitting at home and suddenly Unabomber's face was on the news. Apparently, he was a known arsonist in the area. He had burned down a church and a hotel recently. He had been arrested. The recently burned down hotel was one that he not only lived in but also a place of work where he was supposedly fixing the electrical wires. We slowly turned toward one another with a look of horror on each of our faces. This guy had done extensive electrical work around our house. He gave us a new microwave, toaster, and curling iron. That was the beginning and the ending of Joe's Electrician career.

CHAPTER 11 – DRUG ADDICTION

Not long into Joe and my mom's relationship, when I was 10, mom became pregnant. I felt very lonely as a child and thought that if I only had a sibling, my life could be so much better. Mom considered having an abortion, but I pleaded with her to keep the baby. I surmise that mom wanted to be a teenager forever, or perhaps she never matured beyond the age when trauma struck. I later believed this to be confirmed as true, when she asked her granddaughter to not call her grandma. In that way, I think she wasn't mature enough for kids and a family.

Joe ended up moving in with us. His drug addiction was growing substantially during this time as he began to smoke dope and eventually would shoot up meth. I would find the pipes around the house and whenever I would find them, I would bury them in the yard. It was a little secret of mine, that still makes me smile to this day. The sight of him frantically tearing the house apart to find his ever-disappearing pipe, was priceless! Later, I found Joe's hiding spot for his needles. For years he blamed the needles as belonging to the homeless people who lived with us, however, I later learned they were his. I had later considered fixing up the basement to turn it into an apartment and as I began to clean, I found a hole in the wall and several needles fell out, nearly falling on top of me.

Mom did drugs but she never had a problem (in my opinion). She used drugs recreationally, mostly weed, but never formed an addiction. People like Joe can't function in life until they get their high. The drugs are a coping mechanism for dealing with stress or life in general. I found Joe to be a pain in the ass, mean, and evil until he would take his drug of choice. After smoking dope, Joe was the kindest person around. Drugs changed him into a bearable human being. Joe, in my mind, was definitely addicted. He soon became unable to live or cope without those substances.

He took all kinds of drugs from Vicodin, dope, weed, LSD, morphine; basically, whatever he could get his hands on. Sometimes, it was liquor. He got really into pain killers for a time, but dope was his main drug of choice. I found the crowd he hung with to be liars, thieves, con artists, and all-around sketchy people. I often had items stolen from my bedroom, saw and heard things I shouldn't have, and felt not at all safe in my own home. As the years went on, I pulled deeper and deeper within myself and pushed people farther away, in order to survive. No one really knew the real me and I preferred it that way.

Another problem was that Joe was never faithful to my mom. Joe had a baby face, big eyes, and he knew he was attractive. He was not sly about his indiscretions in the slightest. I once caught him in the garage with a girl just a year older than me. Her mother had committed suicide and she never knew her father. She came from a broken home. Her grandmother had thrown her down the stairs, and it was obvious that she had poor self-esteem. There were a lot of lost girls around our neighborhood who basically survived by living with anyone who would take them in. Another girl I remember, Chrissy, had a father who was a druggie and mother who was a schizophrenic. She was homeless from the age of fourteen on and was forced to drop out of school because she had nowhere to live. She showed up at her dad's house one day. He later got sober, remarried, and had a new family. He would have nothing to do with Chrissy. It was very sad to observe her pine for him and to watch him reject her so coldly. She was alone. We allowed Chrissy to live with us until she started stealing regularly and then she was back out on the streets with nowhere to go. She was forced to drop out of school and found refuge by coupling with an older man when she was a teenager. I've heard rumors that she struggles with meth and makes a living by breaking into people's homes.

When I caught Joe with this girl, he had his tongue down her throat and hand up her skirt. She had a black leather fringe coat with a mini-skirt so short, I could see the crack in her cheeks. Her brown hair was big with the teased-out look and she wore too much makeup. When I mentioned it to him later, he said I was imagining things. "It's in your head. I was just showing her something," he said. He always denied it. He acted like she was disgusting. That was how he played the entire thing off.

Sometimes growing up in dysfunction, you learn that what you *see*, is not really what you are seeing, which can cause a lot of confusion for children. Clearly, he was making out with this girl and lying about it. It is being able to comprehend and see a situation clearly for what it is, and then being unable to state honestly the truth of that situation. It's like saying it is somehow worse than doing it. That is the lie that is maintained. An example is, I was beaten as a child. I know this, and mom knows this. To not say it is better for our family, but by me saying it out loud, that creates hatred because they perceive I am outing them. The dishonesty and lies create confusion about the truth. As a child, I was often torn with what version of the truth should I be telling? It all came down to who I was protecting.

For a time, a homeless man named Steve lived with us. He was on heroin. Mom felt bad for him because his dad died, and Steve used his father's death as an excuse to play the victim. He was a very skilled manipulator and played mom like a fiddle. Mom felt Steve needed to be saved. Steve stole so many things from us, including dishes, silverware, clothes, and even food. He was a disgusting man who never bathed and left piss filled bottles all around the house. Every room he would be in would have a smell that was difficult to remove. Steve became a soft spot for mom over the years. Eventually, Steve partnered up with a prostitute and they went on to have seven children, who were all put into the foster system. Many years later, the youngest of his children, who was rescued from a crack house, was later adopted and we were able to connect through social media. It was amazing to see how something so great could come from such darkness.

One of the homeless women my mother took into our home a few times was named Allie. Somehow Allie had tons of really nice clothes. She stole them from the store and many of them still had tags on them. Allie was one of my favorites, who lived with us over the years. I grew to love her like a big sister. She had a severe drug addiction and no place to live. She had recently gotten out of prison and lost custody of her child. But somewhere inside her heart was a kind woman and I saw that. She had been raped very young and it led her down a series of bad choices, but deep inside she had goodness somewhere amidst all the pain. After she had been raped, her first real boyfriend ended up being a dealer and that's how she got wrapped up into drugs.

She had wild red hair and a huge sassy attitude. She and I spent a lot of time together. We talked a lot and she would let me wear her nice clothes and do my makeup. I was just starting to get into makeup at the time. She would braid my hair, we would talk about boys, and she would spend quality time with me. Sometimes when parties were going, I would go into the basement and hang out with her. One of our things to do was to eat Spaghetti-O's out of the can together.

After living with us for six months, there was a rumor that she had an affair with Joe, although I felt skeptical about the implication. There was an explosive fight between Allie and mom. It was said that she had good drugs and perhaps Joe manipulated her so he could get good drugs. I'm not sure of the truth of what happened.

Mom felt her worth was degraded by his infidelities. She felt that if he could sleep with someone like this homeless woman, that somehow *that* meant mom's worth was diminished. She didn't understand his indiscretions were a character flaw existing within *him* but made it about *her* inadequacy. I felt sad that mom didn't think highly enough of herself to set standards or create boundaries. People treat you the way you allow them to. I learned this concept early on watching her become a doormat for the many men who walked in and out of our lives. She allowed Joe the right to continue violating her honor again and again because she never gave him consequences to his actions. His choices had nothing to do with her worth. She expected him to change instead of her making a change within herself, by kicking him to the curb.

There were other neighborhood girls, one of which he was rumored to have gotten pregnant. People in the neighborhood called her Misses Magoo because she had a very ugly face, squinty eyes, and a large bulbous nose. Chris was a largely built blonde that he slept with and there was also Shawna. Mom was always the constant for him in the middle of all his indiscretions. I worried a lot about the possibility of him giving her a disease, not only with the needle usage but with the promiscuity. We later found that

Joe contracted hepatitis which caused him severe liver issues. This happened most likely from needle usage. He also had passed chlamydia. As a kid, I didn't understand how diseases were transmitted and I worried often about my mom contracting something from him.

It was like living with a tornado and a hurricane under one roof. They were both bat shit crazy. It is said that people tend to be attracted to others who are typically on the same mental and emotional health level. I think the fact that they connected, showcased both of their brokenness. Deep down, mom was a child who wanted to stay young and have excitement in her life. Joe literally was a child who was young and had no plans of growing up any time soon. They both were wild, and their wildness attracted them to one another, and also ironically ended up destroying their relationship. Their similarity pulled them apart in the end. What she wanted of him, she would never do for him either. It was truly a toxic connection and a mess to observe. There were no standards. If something felt

good, it was fair game and that way of thinking seemed

very unstable to me, even as a child.

CHAPTER 12 – PREGNANCY AND ABUSE

During mom's pregnancy, she and Joe fought constantly. Mostly they fought over Joe's infidelities. One night, Joe came home really late and they got into a huge fight. Mom was more than seven months pregnant at the time and visibly showing. Things escalated to violence between them after she accused him of cheating. I was horrified as I watched Joe pull a metal fence pole out from the wire fence outside, storm in the house, and then proceed to beat my mother with it. She had a large purple circle on her back, where he had shoved the rod into her back. After

hours of this screaming and physical fighting, I became

very worried about the baby and tried to talk some sense

into Joe. I noticed his anger flared greater during the times

when he wasn't high. He was more on edge and more

irritated and the drugs would bring him down, into more of

a comatose state. Basically, I felt that he needed to be high

in order to be able to deal with my crazy mom.

He had gotten several good hits to her in the

stomach area. By this point, I knew the baby could be in

danger. Joe didn't make me feel the same fear that the Dane

did. Joe was violent and a druggie, but when he was high,

he was somewhat decent. When he had bouts of sobriety,

he was an evil devil who was cruel beyond measure.

Abstinence made him intolerable.

I asked if we could make sure the baby was okay

and go to the hospital. By this point, mom was completely

battered and bleeding. She had been his punching bag that night and the source of his frustration from lack of drugs. Her fights were mostly with words and he fought with fists. He reluctantly agreed after I pleaded with him for a while to allow her to get checked out by a doctor.

We loaded into mom's 1986 Renault Alliance with mom at the wheel, and me in the back. Mom and Joe fought the entire drive to the hospital, screaming at each other. "No motherfucker, you are not getting away with this," she screamed. "You crazy bitch, I'll get that baby taken from you," he yelled back. This back and forth was mind-numbing. Once we arrived, Joe had changed his mind about letting her go into the ER because she kept provoking and flaming his anger with her words. He became paranoid that she would report to authorities that he had drugs on him. She blatantly said she was going to take him down. I truly felt that these kinds of fights were like foreplay for them. They loved the drama. One minute they were killing each other and the next, they could be heard all throughout the house having loud sex.

He refused to let her out of the vehicle. They continued slapping and punching one another and I was ashamed when the hospital staff came outside to watch them fight. To my horror, the staff did not intervene; this was a show to them, they were enjoying it. All I could think about was the baby. They were physically hitting each other, and the staff just watched laughing at us.

Finally, after what seemed like hours, Joe said he would let her get out of the car. When she stood to get out, he took his giant boot and kicked her in the back. She fell face forward on the hard cement, landing on her belly. I ran to her, thinking of the baby the entire time. I was scared that she would miscarry. When she stood up, her face was cut from the impact of the ground.

As we got inside the ER, both of them were screaming at the top of their lungs. She was saying, "He beat me," and he was screaming, "She's a crack whore." It was all very humiliating, but I was glad that we could find out about the baby finally. My worry had been solely focused on my sibling, not them. As far as I was concerned, they could fight it out, but the baby was innocent.

I just had to get through this moment as I got through a thousand other crappy moments. Fear was real and I felt I cared more than either of them about this child. Joe ended up taking off and left the hospital after security came.

I felt the doctor judge my mom. That irritated me. I felt many people judge her illness including police, doctors, and even therapists. Mental illness is a sickness that doctors are supposed to help treat but mostly I felt they judged. It's like all they saw was white trash, not the ill person inside.

That bothered me. I felt that he should focus on his patient's health, or on the baby inside, not the scene unfolded in the waiting room. The doctor did an ultrasound on mom. Everything ended up being okay and my sister was born in the spring on a bright sunshiny day.

In the spring of 1991, I was ten and my sister was born. *Finally*, I wasn't alone anymore. She was a bright light who was lighting up my hell.

CHAPTER 13 – HELL HOUSE

The tumultuousness of their relationship only got worse over time. If ever there were two people who were truly toxic for one another, it was these two. His drug use continued to escalate to a point where he got high multiple times a day. He would disappear and reappear a much happier version of himself. He began stealing items from my room and started stealing money from mom. He stole necklaces and jewelry. One such time, I recall - I had a few valuable necklaces which my grandmother had given to me. They were in a case inside our bathroom, in the closet.

He went into the bathroom and when he came out, he

looked very shifty and had a guilted expression on his face.

He looked nervous. Mom had the ability to read all of his

flaws perfectly, so she approached him with blunt

accusation.

He took all of the jewelry out of the case and mom

quickly was on to him. She demanded he empty his

pockets, which he refused to do. He ended up emptying all

but one pocket and they had a stand-off. At his refusal to

budge, she then turned to me and began screaming how this

entire thing was *my* fault. "Why did you leave the jewelry

in the bathroom? You knew he would take it." I couldn't

believe she was blaming me for this idiot's decision. This is

part of the dysfunctional family thing. Blame anyone

except for the wrongdoer. Then you create overly

responsible victims and non-responsible criminals. Once a

person takes responsibility, then they must *change* and that is exactly why no one wants to take responsibility. He didn't want to change.

This, unfortunately, wasn't the first accusation mom made with me, regarding him. Joe was a man whore. He was not shy about his love for sex. I honestly think he would have had sex with literally every person if he could. There were rumors that he frequented prostitutes and cheated on my mom several times. Girlfriends were passed around between brothers and friends. Eventually, mom became jealous even of me, her ten-year-old daughter. One night, I was reading in my closet. I loved to read in my closet because honestly, it was the quietest place in the house. In reaching for my book, above the hangers, I found a stack of polaroid pictures. I noticed they were all naked pictures of Joe, strewn out in various sexual poses. I nearly gagged at the sight of them with his legs spread open and his penis in his hand. I stormed out into the living room, throwing them at mom. "What in the hell are these doing in my room?" I demanded. It was creepy and inappropriate. It disgusted me. I let them have it. Joe also left condoms filled with semen in my room, which really grossed me out. She turned on me saying, "I know you've been fucking him. You ain't no virgin.... I know," she said with a psychotic tone like she was in on some secret. I was ten at the time and hadn't yet gotten my period, let alone had sex. Because of the openness of sexuality and orgies which went on in my house, I vowed at an early age to only give myself to one man. It wasn't a religious thing it was a dignity thing. All of the drugs and overly sexual environment completely turned me away from wanting anything to do with that type of lifestyle. At this, she began accusing me of seducing and sleeping with him. It was a preposterous and ridiculous notion. It left me speechless and near laughter. As she cornered me into the wall, she began hitting my face. Her anger was building and I was being lit on fire. I put my arms up to defend myself. It was hard to have restraint with her, but I understood that she thrived on the atmosphere of chaos and drama. If I were to engage with her in any way, it would just keep escalating. She seemed to love the drama whereas I detested it. I absorbed a lot as a child, in order to keep the peace and to deescalate insanely crazy situations. Over the years, I became quite skilled in shutting down the drama and in growing my peacemaker skills. My typical tool was silence and walking away if I was able. However, she wouldn't let me leave.

Suddenly, her screams drastically changed to cries for help toward Joe. She wasn't letting me leave even though I tried desperately to get away from her. She began telling Joe, "She hit me, Joe. She hit me!" "I literally did not lay a finger on her," I said. I *knew* her manipulation. Her intent was to get Joe in on the fight against me. This way, they could both come against me, and I would be the new punching bag for the night. This would all be at their amusement as they enjoyed the drama. And, it worked. He fell for it.

Joe came in shoving me and calling me a few curse words. "What did you fucking do?" he screamed at me with malice. Now he was the savior and I was the evil child in this ridiculous story! It was always drama with these two. They wouldn't know how to conjure up peace if their lives depended on it. He eventually pinned me to the ground where the two of them sat on top of me. I remember her laughing at the control she had over me and she took pleasure in sitting on my chest. This was fun for her. I felt suffocated and powerless to move. I felt bullied. To this day, I cannot handle people pinning me down.

The situation continued to escalate until the police got called and I ended up leaving the house with a relative. I wished I would never have to go back, but I knew better.

My plan, my entire life was to get the hell out of that house. I dreamed about it, thought about it, planned it, wrote it, and prayed it. I *could not wait* to leave that house.

It wasn't long after, the next-door neighbor started having an affair with Joe. Crystal was married but Joe didn't care. He had no ability to deny his lustful urges. They openly showed affection for one another and he flaunted the affair in my mother's face. It crushed her completely. Crystal was much younger than my mom and much more beautiful. She had breast implants, was skinny, and dressed provocatively. She wasn't much older than I was (at nineteen) and looked like she could've been a model.

It started when mom invited the new neighbor over to one of our parties. From there, we went to their house to have a barbeque. Soon, the neighbors became fast friends. It was a dangerous situation because, during one of their parties, a friend had been gang-raped at their house. It was clear these were not good people. As I got older, I pulled more and more toward myself and tried to find places to escape outside the home.

At the discovery of the affair, I remember mom taking the entire drawer of Joe's clothes and setting fire to every piece of clothing he owned in our front yard. She also dragged out his furniture setting that ablaze as well. We had a huge bonfire in our yard and roasted marshmallows over Joe's burned clothes. Mom threw a small party and they poured beer onto the fire in celebration.

After the pile turned to ash, mom then called Joe on the phone saying, "Come get your shit." When Joe showed up, he was horrified to see a charred pile of ash where some of his most memorable items were destroyed. His trademark leather hat, he had since middle school was destroyed, along with his leather jacket, and a piece of furniture was completely burned. Mom not only laughed in his face but continued to laugh for days over this. She had a

wicked laugh and felt satisfied at the hurt she caused him.

She loved the expression that was on his face and felt

vindicated by her revenge.

CHAPTER 14 – BAR NIGHTS

When I was twelve, Joe left and mom started going
to the bar more often. Every night I would be with the baby
and mom would be out with friends getting drunk and
loaded. A few times she brought me to the bar with her,
where I stayed in the car with the baby, but I preferred to
stay home.

One night, I was home alone with the baby
watching reruns of Cheers. Joe had been out of our lives for

a few weeks. Mom was out. Suddenly, Joe kicked open the front door. He had a look of rage on his face and stared at me in silence. I had never seen Joe look so filled with fury, and I was certain that he was on a dangerous drug he had not taken before. He was someone else entirely at that moment and I did not recognize him. That old familiar heart race and shallow breathing came back to me in an instant.

The baby was asleep in the crib and I just sat motionless on the couch, waiting for him to make a move. It was his move, after all, in this game of chess we were playing. The phone was near me because I had been talking to a friend earlier that night. He launched for the phone, tearing it from the side of my lap. With that, he began to bash his face against the phone in front of me over and over, never losing eye contact with me. It was an old rotary phone and he continued smashing the phone against his face until blood was pouring out from his face. He continued until the phone disintegrated and his face was a bloody mess of cuts and gashes. He had a two by four piece of wood with him and he proceeded to break everything in the house in front of me. I watched as he broke picture frames, the television, the lamp, the fish tank, and everything in his path. I was frozen, stuck to the couch, trying to claim my breath and come up with a plan that didn't involve me being beaten. I didn't want to move because I thought that he would hurt or kill me. Aside from the occasional push, shove, or scream sessions, he hadn't truly taken his violence out on me with fists. I had watched him physically hurt my mother, however, usually after she provoked him heavily.

Just then, with a frantic look on his face, he ran to the basement. It was as if his attention shifted. I later discovered that the basement ceiling was one of the places he kept his drugs hidden. I knew this moment was my opportunity.

It was then that I remembered one of the homeless people who was living in our basement was down there now, Steve. I began to hear screaming in the basement. It was a high-pitched scream and Steve was begging Joe for his life. "Stop Joe!", he screamed. "Stop!" It sounded like Joe was killing him. There were crashes and sounds of things breaking along with this man's pleading cries.

I tiptoed quickly to the bedroom and grabbed the baby. I ran out the front door as fast as I could with the baby in my arms, into the night, convinced he was just a step behind me. The door slammed behind me and I thought I heard him coming. I was panicked to get out of there fast.

All the lights were out on the street and I wasn't sure where to go. I didn't even have shoes on and the baby wasn't wrapped in a blanket. I wondered whose door I should knock on. No matter what house I approached that night, I was going to wake my neighbor up. It was definitely past midnight.

I ended up going to our neighbor Mel's house. Mel was a former army vet who lost two legs. He was now a frail old man, but to me, he was always exceptionally kind. Mel kept an eye on me and was a sort of comfort throughout the years. He wasn't a huge presence, but I know he watched over me. I felt that my sister and I would be safe over at Mel's place.

I knocked aggressively while staring across the street at my front door. I was afraid Joe would come for us any minute now. It took a while for Mel to come.

Mel came to the door in his wheelchair with his PJs on and his hair a rat's nest. I had clearly woken him out of sleep. I felt horrible and apologized as I entered his house. I immediately smelled the smoke waft out his door. Mel was a chain smoker and his entire house reeked of smoke. Once, he fell asleep while smoking and the fire department had to come because he nearly burned his house down. Mel was also a hoarder and his house smelled very badly. It was an odd uncleanly smell of body odor, feces, pets, urine, and cigarettes. He wasn't a clean man, but he had a kind heart. I told him quickly what had happened, and then he immediately called the police.

CHAPTER 15 - PRISON

When the police came, Joe was arrested. There were several cop cars outside our house as they walked him to the car. An ambulance arrived and Steve was wheeled out. I couldn't tell if he was alive. Joe tried to say that the homeless man did the destruction to his face, however, my story did not align with Joe's. The phone had blood on it, Steve was beaten within an inch of his life and ultimately the police believed the version I provided, of him bashing his face against the phone.

Steve was seriously hurt, and Joe was not going to get out of this. Joe hoped that I would lie for him to the court so his sentence would be shortened. He ended up being sentenced to prison. He had beat the homeless man within an inch of his life. Steve's entire face was swollen, and he was in the hospital for some time. I am not sure if the drugs were missing, or if he was just high on something which made him insane that night, but I saw a side to Joe I had never seen before, and it terrified me.

I could finally breathe a sigh of relief at the thought of possibly having some peace in our lives now that Joe was going to prison. He was charged with breaking and entering and assault. There were drug charges also. As the drugs escalated and became more of a necessity for him, he was becoming more frightening and unpredictable. I was glad he was going to prison. I hoped that we could have some quiet in our house now that he was gone.

Joe asked my mother if I would lie on his behalf so that he would get a lesser prison sentence. Because of my mom's resentment and his infidelities, she would not budge in the slightest.

While in prison, Joe said he, "found the Lord." He said he would read his Bible for hours and he even wrote letters, talking about his new-found faith. I thought this was great news and that he was changing. He made promises to take us all to church and to read the Bible together. It was during this same time, that I myself began going to a church with a friend. It started out as a free meal thing and then turned into a boy crush thing, and I ended up finding comfort within the walls of the church.

The people in the church were very unlike me, and I felt a plethora of emotions while there. Sometimes I felt envious of their seemingly perfect lives. Sometimes I felt uncomfortable with how much I did *not* fit in with these people. My life was a mess. Yet somehow, I felt comforted as well, like maybe God was real, and He had access to me in those few hours every Sunday. There were families who were all together and they seemed happy. I didn't see drug addicts or mental cases in the church, and I wondered if there was something to this "God thing". Maybe people who know God are not crazy, I thought. Maybe people who know God are truly happy inside. That's when the exploration began of my own faith.

I would watch the families in the church, and my heart would ache with a deep longing for a family of my own and a deeper connection. Keep in mind, I didn't have true parents and I didn't have the support system I craved. I felt very much on my own from early childhood mentally, financially, and physically. In watching these families interact, it showed me that another life was possible.

Joe continued to improve and worked his program while serving his prison sentence. It seemed very promising. The family attended Narconon/Alanon meetings. Soon Joe was in a half-way house located a few hours outside of Des Moines. The family would visit him, and he looked so much better as time went on. His body was drug-free and he even began to grow muscle. The color of his skin looked pinker and less gray. I had never seen him look so good. His mind seemed clearer. His thoughts seemed more organized and less erratic. For the first time, Joe would talk about the future. He never did that. It was always about the next party, the next scam, or the next con. To hear him talk about his desire to preach and that he wanted to get his GED, made me feel very happy for him. I couldn't wait to start our new life with this new Joe.

Eventually, Joe got out on house arrest for good behavior. He had made good friends with the prison

Chaplain and even said he wanted to be a preacher someday.

I remember the first day his bracelet was removed. I thought perhaps there is a new Joe in our midst. I thought it would be a new beginning for all of us and his change will cause all of us to change for the better. He visually looked different and constantly talked about God.

That first day, he was using drugs again. I remember our conversation. He said, "Did you really believe all that God bullshit?" I looked at him puzzled. "You are a dumb mother-fucker, aren't you?" he said. He went on to tell me that he *used* the God thing as a tool of manipulation so he could get out of prison on good behavior. It was all a lie and he was as much an atheist as he's ever been. Nothing had changed. Nothing inside him had changed. He was the same manipulative lying man. My heart sank at this realization. This was all a game and we were fooled.

I knew that my family was absolutely screwed up and I felt that the church would be a good decision and a good place to help teach *me* what family is and what "normal" is. I figured normal families didn't do drugs, get arrested, or do criminal activity together. Literally every interaction with my family was jacked up in more ways than mentionable and I craved a boring life of normality. I gravitated toward stability even though that was foreign.

When you grow up in dysfunction, what seems normal to you is definitely not normal to the rest of the world. An example would be, when my future husband and I got into our first argument, I shrunk on the floor and covered my face shielding myself from him. He was hurt that I had recoiled. He couldn't believe I would ever think that he would hit me. He didn't understand that hitting was very normal in our home. There were no real boundaries in our house. There was never a dignity line that was upheld and not crossed. Everything was fair game and playing dirty, crossing lines, being disrespectful, cheating, stealing, and being criminal was a way of life. It was normal. You fuck me over and I will fuck you over harder– that was the mentality. All of us were damaged survivors in a messed-up world doing whatever we had to do to endure. Play the game or *get played* because the game is going whether you realize it or not. It's a world of manipulation with a lot of land mines, and you have to watch your back constantly. That dysfunctional mentality is real. Once you live it, it's all you know. You learn to critique everyone. You are constantly in fight mode and the world is against you. That's what it felt like in my childhood. It is hard to unlearn those patterns and mentalities.

In our family lying was normal. We all protected mom's secret for years. We hid the truth of what was really happening in our house. As I said, to do a bad thing, is perceived as less *impacting* as "saying" the bad thing. It's the secrets that make us sick. To speak about it is to shine a light on it.

Like I said, in the church, I felt very out of place. If these people only knew some of the stuff I had been dealing with at home, I thought. I'd be judged. I knew they would criticize me. I knew they wouldn't understand. I hid it. This hell thing they talk a lot about sounded like my *house*.

Joe did a second stint in prison. This time it was over a robbery. He wasn't out for very long before he went back in. A few of his friends decided to rob a gas station and apparently there was a patrol car watching the area. He was in prison until I was age fifteen.

Joe was a character that is hard, to sum up. He had an ability within, where he was an exceptional charmer. He could completely fool people. It always amazed me how people would fall under his allure when *I* knew better. He was very charismatic, handsome, and social. But he used all of his appeals simply to get what he wanted. At his core, he was a manipulator and a liar. I saw past his charade; I saw the real him on the inside. He would confuse my mom because he could play the chameleon so convincingly. He fluxed between mystifying, frightening, exciting, fun, and violent. He could be explosive, bring amusement, cause confusion, and cause people to go into survival-mode. It was manipulation. He could change the dynamic, making you feel comfortable, then uncomfortable, confused, or vulnerable always gaining the upper hand. He could sell people on the *belief* that he truly changed when really it was all an act. That manipulation was damaging for me, with my pre-existing trust issues. What complicates my feelings about Joe is that we had some fun moments together. He was high on dope and our lives were in shambles, but there were fun times in the midst of craziness.

One of those funny moments involved him hanging a punching bag. He ended up tearing the entire ceiling out of our house because he didn't anchor it to a stud. His stupidity sometimes provided much-needed comedic relief. Once, he took me to steal food from a Boys and Girls Club. Volunteering at the Boys and Girls Club was part of his parole. I didn't want to steal the food and refused to join in. I stood there while he loaded pile after pile into the dumpster. His plan was to act as if he was taking out the trash, when really, he was stealing food. He planned to come back after midnight, jump in the dumpster, and bring the food home. Watching him at midnight, dive into that dumpster, I couldn't help but laugh when his head popped up out of the dumpster and he pulled out grocery bags of food. Another time, at the Iowa State Fair, mom jokingly said, I like those Coca Cola umbrellas. He said, "What my baby wants, my baby gets." At that, he ripped it out of the table and carried that umbrella several blocks back to our house. Again, it was criminal but the dumb stuff he did provided a sense of comedy.

Another time, we went sledding at Grandview. I threw a snowball at him, which ended up being ice. His face was cut badly. Sometimes we laughed about violent things. It's dysfunctional and crazy, but that was our life. He and I joked about my crazy mom and we would share hilarious stories, laughing about all the stuff we endured with her. Sometimes, he felt like a brother.

Once we took off hiking into the woods and got completely lost. It started raining, then turned to hail, then we heard the tornado sirens. Hours later, covered in mud and completely soaked we found our way out of the woods; we laughed about it all night. It was stupid but funny.

Another time, he decided to glue mirrors to our ceiling (for what I can only assume to be his sexual pleasures with my mother). It took him hours to glue the mirrors and all night, pieces of glass were shattering all around us. We literally woke up in blood, and his face was cut because he didn't use superglue. We laughed at his stupidity, even though we were covered in blood.

There was also the time we got fleas really bad in our house and all the popular "party" kids from my school needed a place to crash for the night until the drugs wore off. They came to Joe because he was the cool guy who wouldn't tell their parents or judge. Literally all night the kids were screaming, slapping their legs, and shouting about how torturous it was to sleep with fleas. They all promised they would never get high again. Joe and I thought this was such a great cure for drugs and laughed all night.

One of the funnier memories I have with him was our first Christmas together. Mom was notorious for her cheap ways, and we couldn't afford a Christmas tree. Somehow, he managed to gather a bunch of spare fake tree limbs from the thrift store and various places. Most of them didn't fit on the wire inside our fake tree, so there were very large holes and gaps in the tree. He attempted to tie them with string. To me it was obvious this was a fail, but to mom and him, we could totally make this work. They proceeded to get out sewing thread and tightly wound it around the tree. After all the decorations were in place, you truly couldn't tell this tree was jerry-rigged. We laughed about our ghetto Christmas tree for years to come.

Mom said for years she wanted an exercise bike. As I said, my family wouldn't buy things new. Joe found an exercise bike on the curb in front of a house beside their garbage and brought it home to mom as a surprise. We died laughing when we realized the bike was made for a little person, and Joe got stuck on the bike and was unable to get off because his knees were touching his lips.

Once mom bought a vacuum for $2 which would not come out of the upright position. We had such frustration over trying to vacuum the floor while the vacuum was locked upright that we resorted to getting on our hands and knees to pick up the crumbs! It was funny at the time because of mom's extreme cheap ways.

Once I wanted to learn the guitar and mom found a guitar on the curb of someone's house. It had two strings and was duck taped at the top. She thought this was an exceptional find, but it was obviously garbage. She thought it could be fixed with tape and while I strung the guitar, one more string came loose. Joe and I laughed hysterically over this.

All these things make my feelings about Joe very complex. I both loved and hated him and that's the truth.

Eventually, Joe succumbed to the demon that was his addiction and it led him to death's door. His temptation came in the form of a woman. She had no boundaries and led him to heroin. She came with a promise. She came with seduction. She came with beauty. He fell into her, eventually, it cost him everything. He became homeless and went missing for more than a decade. It is rumored that he was killed.

CHAPTER 16 - HOMICIDE

By the age of thirteen, I became very skilled at reading people. I had to learn from a young age to constantly scan the environment because I never knew what was coming next. Life was one crisis to the next, and I literally did not know what to expect from one day to the next. Because of that, I later married a very stable man who is arguably boring; which by the way is his best quality if you ask me!

While Joe was in prison the second time, mom continued her partying ways. I stayed home with my young sister while mom went out nearly every night to blow off steam. Mom brought strange men to our home and we had a few scary moments. One time in 1993, when I was around the age of twelve mom and her best friend Sandy went to a bar about five blocks from our house. Mom and Sandy were best friends from childhood. Sandy had been married to a man with whom she was very unhappy. He had been abusing her physically and she finally got the courage to leave. She was recently single and wanted to go out, party, and meet men. Sandy's two daughters (Andy and Cammie) were my close friends and I babysat the young Andy. They had a "Screw our ex's" mentality between the two of them. Both women felt cheated by the men in their lives, so they went out and had a good time together. They were wild, unchained, and fearless.

Mom met a guy named Terry at the bar. She and

Terry struck up a conversation and he started buying her

drinks. At the bar, Terry's friend Rick got with my mom's

friend Sandy. The four of them partied all night, drank

beer, and danced. It was a night of harmless fun. Not long

after, Sandy left with Rick and mom brought Terry to our

house for a one-night stand. I was told not to come into the

living room until morning. Sometimes when I couldn't

leave the room, I would have urine cups. I could hear the

music and the sound of them having sex. At least they

warned me, I thought. I cranked up my music louder to

drown them out. Eventually, Terry would be too boring for

mom. She grew very bored with men who weren't wild like

her.

We found out later that Rick, the man Sandy had

gone home with, was involved in a drug deal gone wrong.

It was a famous case in Iowa. Rick was set to testify in

court against a mob man. No one knew this except for

Rick. That night at the bar, both Sandy and Rick were being watched and they were followed home. When Sandy got home, her two daughters Cammie and Andy were tucked into bed, fast asleep. She had relatives all around her neighborhood, so it was thought that the house was very safe.

Sandy and Rick heard a knock at the door and that's when the nightmare began. They never saw it coming. A stranger tied up the entire family and tortured them. We discovered later from an informant that Sandy had pleaded for her life and the lives of her two daughters, but the killer had no regard for her life or the lives of her children. Both Rick and Sandy were murdered in front of the children. It was said that the children wouldn't stop screaming so he silenced them also, by wrapping a tight cord around each of their necks.

Rick, Sandy, her two daughters, Andy age 6, and Cammie age 10 were murdered that night in Sandy's home in Iowa. All four were buried, in a field and forest in southwest Mason City, Iowa. Later a fifth person was killed. Their disappearance impacted our lives tremendously. That was mom's best friend, and we didn't know for several years the truth of what happened that night.

Sandy just happened to pick the wrong person. She had no idea that this man would cause the annihilation of her entire family. He had no idea the scope of the situation he was involved in. It was tragic and a loss for us and so many others. These precious lives were taken senselessly.

The thought passed through our minds, what if mom picked the other guy? That could have been us, easily. This tragedy calmed her partying down quite a bit. She still went out and still partied, but she definitely wasn't as wild. The situation put a little more fear inside of her.

I think often about Sandy and her girls. I think of what they might have become and what they would look like today. I remember Sandy's laugh, Cammie's perky voice, and the smell of the lilacs in their yard.

CHAPTER 17 – HIDING IN CHURCH

My life became church-centered after the age of
fourteen. I used the church as a coping mechanism to
escape my poor home life. I looked for ways to not be
home. Mom's mental breakdowns continued and as time
passed, it seemed the spells became worse and stayed
longer. I didn't know if it damaged her brain, but it felt like
it was degenerative. It was very difficult to deal with,
especially as I started my period and began my teen years. I
was dealing with hormones and trying to parent my own

mother. I felt I needed help but also needed to help her. It was a hard time.

When she had Joe in her life, I felt she had something to put her focus on. She was still crazy, but *he* received the brunt of it. Now that he was in prison, *I* was the lucky winner. I got her screams, her hits, her accusations, and endless drama. Truthfully, she wore me out.

She mocked me relentlessly for going to church. She told me I would never fit in with these phonies and that none of them were genuine people. I didn't believe her. I'm thankful for the role church played in my life during this turbulent time because it gave me a sense of sanity and also helped form a sense of normality as I didn't always know healthy from dysfunctional.

One night after church got out, I came home to find

every item in our home was gone. Mom was a hoarder so I

stood speechless in our living room completely baffled as

to where all the items in our house could have gone. The

couch, the piano, the file cabinet, the table, the television,

the lamp – it was all gone. The entire living room was bare.

I felt confused for a few moments. I found mom in one of

the back bedrooms. She had a butter knife and was tearing

at the drywall. I watched her destroy the walls, feeling

confused. "Where are our things, mom?" She mumbled to

herself and said some gibberish. I continued pressing her.

Eventually, she told me that she gave everything away to a

girl who would appreciate it. "You are a spoiled bitch," she

told me frankly, while still ferociously digging at the

drywall. I felt shocked, stunned, and unsure of how to

respond. I felt it was always the good nights at church,

those were the nights her devil came out to play. Reacting

was the worst thing I could do so my response was silence.

I had to learn how to have no reaction, which was hard as a child. I did what came most natural to me and that was to call my grandparents.

By this point, they were in their 80s. They had spent their *entire* lives dealing with her breakdowns and it visibly showed. Every wrinkle, every exhausted exhale; it showed in their tired eyes. My grandparents were truly incredible people. They raised their kids right and worked as a team together. They ran a successful business for 40 years and loved each other. I never understood why people as good as them, were dealt with such painful blows in life. It is true, it rains on the just and the unjust.

When my grandparents arrived, mom became violent. She hated people interfering with her mental health. Her violent tendencies continued to escalate as the years went on. Her deep hatred for the mental hospital and for her family for putting her there grew. We ended up finding all of our things. They were thrown into a large pile down the basement stairs. There was a massive heaping pile.

She came after my grandmother physically, once grandma tried to strongarm her into getting help. Mom was placed into the mental hospital. By this point, I was old enough and responsible enough to care for my sister. My grandparents would make sure we had food, but I did my own thing for the most part and didn't require supervision.

I was already a parent to mom, but I became a parent to my sibling. I took her to school and picked her up. I prepared breakfast, lunch, and dinner. She came with me everywhere including out with friends, church, the library, the store, and later on dates. It sounds selfish but I resented having to be a parent so young to my sibling. I loved her but it felt unfair and I wanted to be a normal teenager who didn't have to tote a child around. (This is part of the reason

I waited so long to have children. Being a parent to her made me grasp and understand the reality that involved being a mother.)

A decade later, my grandmother died. There are some within our family that feel that mom may have been the cause of her death. Their relationship was fraught with tension mom's entire life. It was also known that during spells, mom would become physically violent and later have no recollection of the event. During my grandmother's last days, I visited back home from out of state. I was horrified to see bugs covering the kitchen counter and my grandfather sitting in soiled clothing, which visibly had fecal stains on it. They were extraordinarily clean people, so this was highly alarming and concerning. The food on their plates was swarming with small bugs. At that time, mom was taking care of them and she was not adept or capable to care for them properly. I brought my concerns to family members and proceeded to catch my flight back home. This was out of my control as I no longer lived at home, but I did what I could for them.

I was told that the family tried to remove mom from the house. She fell apart badly around the time grandma was very sick. Several items of value had gone missing. My relative left to the pharmacy to pick up medication and grandma was fine before he left. When he returned twenty minutes later, she was lying with her face in the pillow and mom was in the middle of an episode, standing over her pacing back and forth. She said something along the lines of, "I helped her go. She wanted to go." We don't know what happened, but some within our family feel mom may have been responsible. It's hard to say.

CHAPTER 18 – THE BOY WITH THE SPIKY HAIR

I began saving my money at fourteen so that I could move away the day I graduated high school. I had been planning this and as the time approached, my anticipation grew. I required an adult to open a bank account and at one-point mom got into my savings, stealing it. She refused to give it back. I had to call another relative to help lock her out of my account. She argued that it was legally hers because I was minor. Also, she felt I owed her room and board. She said frequently that I was spoiled, and my life was too easy, however, I never saw it that way. My grandparents bought the home and mom lived there free. She collected welfare and often complained about my deadbeat father not supporting her. We were very poor, and I felt bad that she struggled, but didn't agree with her about my life as being easy. She truly hated my father and sometimes I thought she hated me because I reminded her of him.

My family guilt-tripped me a lot by saying I was mom's guardian and responsible for her mental health. "What will happen to her when you leave?" they would say. "She's going to be on the street!" I watched my grandparents spend their entire lives putting the (bowling) bumpers up for her and I watched her slowly drain them of their life. Ultimately, all their sacrifices did not cure her. It did, however, help me. For that, I am grateful.

I was selfish at fourteen, but I decided I'm not going to sacrifice my sanity, future, and life for a person who doesn't care to be well. If she wants to drive her life off a cliff, how can I stop her? *All* I thought about, was escaping. Thoughts of leaving Iowa consumed me.

During the mid-'90s and at the age of fourteen, while in the church I met a boy. The first time I saw him, was in the front foyer of the church. He stood next to a thin blonde and I noticed his enormous eyes. I assumed that he and the girl were an item and didn't think much about it. The girl wasn't model beautiful in her face, but she had a nice figure. She had thin lips and thin blonde hair. Her eyes reminded me of Susan Sarandon. This girl stood out because her clothes were tight.

A friend invited me to church. She was unlike anyone our age. I tended to gravitate toward unique people. She liked to wear clothes that her grandmother patched and liked really old-fashioned music, such as the Gaithers. She would blast this music in the car, and I would shrink in the seat in embarrassment. Her uniqueness is what made her so different from anyone else. I liked that she didn't fit the mold. Most people found her odd and one time, someone suggested she and I were lovers, and we had a good laugh over that. We were the odd squad. I was awkward and 100% a virgin, with not even kissing experience at age fourteen. The only date I had, was with a boy from Louisiana who left me at the arcade after I ran out of money. Oddball Sam had dated a boy for four years who was five years older than her. She broke things off recently and he was devastated. He was very much in love with her, but I found it weird because she was in junior high (at age 14) and he had graduated high school (age 19). I didn't understand what they had in common. He reminded me of the lead singer of the band Beck. His hair was blonde and greasy, he was tall and gangly, and he had a creepy awkward way about him. She wanted to be young and see what else was out there. She resented his neediness. My quirky friend liked a boy in the church who had some drama unfolding. This curly-haired waif dated a girl for several years named Alison. Her family was going through a messy separation and she was struggling to come to terms with the divorce. Sam's crush, Ian, ended things with her painfully and publicly, which I found to be low. He was flirty which I felt was insensitive to Alison. Eventually, Ian hooked up with the pastor's daughter Mandy, who was nowhere near as beautiful. Alison had hair in ringlets, perfect skin, and dimples. Mandy was shaped like a tree trunk and had eyes that were too far apart. I didn't see what Sam saw in him.

I enjoyed this church because every week there were fun events. The Pastor engaged everyone. We dribbled basketballs around the sanctuary, hopped, crawled, and acted fun things out. Also, I loved the escape.

It was the age where I noticed boys. My friend wanted Ian horribly while I pined for brown-eyed-Spiky. I was analyzing him. I thought Sam might be a little sadistic to go for Ian but luckily, we didn't have the same taste in boys. I liked awkward, shy, geeky, big-eyed, guys with large eyebrows and large noses. Being a good person was essential. She liked the obvious guys that *everyone* liked and gravitated toward jerks. At the time, grunge was big, and she went for grungy boys whereas I liked the clean-cut ones. Spiky was shy but had an attraction that many girls liked. He wasn't the quarterback, but he wasn't the band geek either. He was somewhere in the middle.

Week after week, Spiky and blondie sat together so I kept my crush tendencies under control. Spiky was a big topic of conversation in the girl's restroom. It seemed that most of the girls in the church had a thing for this boy, including one of the most beautiful girls Amber. Amber was stunning and looked a lot like Elizabeth Hurley. Based on the bathroom conversation, I learned that he came from a good family, went to a private Christian school, his parents lived near Grandview in a middle-class home, and his family attended church. Someone said that his mother was a nurse. His parents had been married for years and he had a few sisters. I felt he was out of my league, but I still tantalized the thought of dating him. Understand there was a theme of rejection in my life that permeated my mind. I wasn't paid much attention to, so my teenage thoughts about myself were exiguous.

From the age of fourteen to seventeen, he was my crush. While powdering my nose, I blatantly asked the blonde Sarandon lookalike if they were an item. She said no and smiled slyly at me.

I discovered that Spiky liked the outdoors and wanted to be a forest ranger. As I said, girls talked about him constantly and I watched and listened. I also liked the outdoors. My dream was to live in the woods with a mountain view. I would hike trails and nature became a place of escape for me. I went on hikes, fished, and liked to get lost in the woods. I felt we shared a love of nature and the outdoors, in addition to sharing our faith and both had perfectionistic, reserved, and cautious personalities. But to be honest, it was his eyes. There was just that slight problem of my dysfunctional family.

We all have a high school crush and he was mine. We had a very fun youth group that went to the waterpark, bowling, went out to eat, and did camping retreats. There was *always* something fun going on. *It kept me out of my house.* During one of the church services, Spiky was picked on by the pastor. He was blindfolded in front of the entire church and forced to walk on something mushy and gross. I noticed his florescent white feet that had never seen the light of day and his extraordinarily hairy legs. It made me giggle. He had to guess what the substance was in between his toes, and the point of the message was that we can see without the blindfold better. I could tell this was very painful for him. He was not the kind of person who liked a lot of attention drawn to himself and his face got very red. His embarrassment was adorable. I saw him as being so perfect that it was nice seeing him be uncomfortable. I'm not sadistic, but I enjoyed this moment because he seemed less god-like and more human. Being on stage or in front of people never phased me, even though I was shy in one on one conversation.

His eyes were his best feature, but his hair was his thing. He had a closely shaved neck and face. He was over six feet tall and he had slight lined dimples on either cheek with white teeth and a kind smile. He was thin, handsome, quiet, and respectful. There was a coyness about his persona and his eyes entered a room before he did.

I noticed he always wore a watch and was very punctual, clean, and polished. For people our age, he seemed overly responsible and adult-like.

Week after week, I looked forward to seeing this boy. I admired him from afar while my friend continued to have a thing for Ian. Spiky's eyes covered much of his face and they had this effect of making me feel seen and exposed, which made me feel uncomfortable, excited, and made my stomach flip. His eyes were like two planets glued on his face. You couldn't help but stare and you couldn't tell where his iris and pupil began and ended. The blackness of his eyes made them appear even bigger. I don't know what it is about humans and creatures with large eyes, but they are adorable (for example Gizmo, Yoda, and Tarsiers). They were runway lights that demanded your focus. It didn't matter which part of the room he was facing; he had these eyes that seemed to suck you into his orbit. I was a person who liked to *hide*, and his eyes would *find* me and pull me out.

The church was a bubble utopia where everyone seemed happy and loving. All the families hugged, everyone was kind, and people smiled. Fights didn't break out, people didn't cuss, or act insane. It felt safe.

I was only fourteen and didn't have any experience with boys. I was clueless to how the opposite sex worked. My only experience was with that of mom's crazy boyfriends, Joe's perverted friends, and the *one* time my cousin brought me to a pool party, where most of the people were making out, while I read a book. I considered myself a shy introvert. I felt that if I were to date, I would need to find someone who understood (at least in part) the dysfunction that was my life. There was *no* way it would have worked otherwise. For me dating was a minefield because I had secrets which were messy; secrets which were both mine and not mine. I didn't always feel safe in sharing these, because I felt I'd be judged. One of the first conversations any boy would strike up while on a date is, "So tell me about your family." I kept all my dirty laundry hidden. I felt ashamed of my home life.

I liked this boy, but there was a great disparity. I believed he would *never* understand my life, my past, *or* my crazy family. It was a crush. He was a Mount Everest in his character, looks, and excellent family. He felt unreachable. In my mind, he was a perfectly chiseled statue with God-made eyes. I was fourteen, born in a mess and he was sixteen and seemed to have life figured out. I felt like Andie in the movie Pretty in Pink. He was Blane. Our social statuses were uneven. We shared similar interests, but we were born from two different worlds.

Normal and sane intimidated me. I didn't know what normal *was* in any sense and I felt out of my element with this boy.

I never let myself get too lost in my crush because of all of my ambivalences about our social differences. It's complicated having to explain, why you have to maintain boundaries with your mother. For people who have never dealt with addiction or dysfunction, this might seem cruel. However, *boundaries* are the only way to maintain a sense of peace. Dysfunctional people wreak havoc. Ultimately - is a toxic person worth having in your life and if so, how close should you allow them to be? This brings questions about, which aren't always easy. Understand that the person beyond the illness is my mom and I love her very much, regardless of her issues. However, the truth is that her illness is difficult for others. That was the complicated relationship I had with my mother. It was not at all simple and most certainly was not black and white.

194

Could Spiky have handled seeing her living in filth, the cockroaches, the breakdowns, the drugs, the openness of sexuality, the police, or how my mother was truly my kryptonite? She had the power to break me easily and did often. Was Spiky's character strong enough to withstand *her* issues and *my* weakness to her? I didn't know boundaries. Also, her issues created broken trust in me. I hadn't received enough exposure to be able to discern health from dysfunction. For a boyfriend to take on an ill parent *and* a broken girlfriend is a lot, keeping in mind he was only a teenager. I had to grow up quickly but most kids my age did not, and that discrepancy was challenging. I required maturity.

All of these thousands of thoughts circled in my mind. It was like being chained to a situation you desperately want to escape from. My past was part of me, and I couldn't remove it. All that he had seen up until that point was his small Christian utopia whereas I had seen it

195

all. There is a fundamental difference between someone living in trauma versus someone not. A person who lives in suffering is wired for protection whereas free people live unafraid. Fear-based thoughts are not a reality for people who have never lived with trauma. Perceptions, realities, and experiences are unevenly matched, and that divide is hard to bridge.

I say all this because I was highly stressed about dating. I was *afraid* of allowing people close enough to me, to *see the pain* of my reality. I didn't feel anyone could be trusted with that. What if Spiky had laughed at my ill mother? What if he became repulsed by our home or the smell of it? What if she made him feel afraid? I didn't think he would understand my situation. I overthought it horribly.

During a church event, we had all night sleep-ins, went camping, had parties, and ate out. Going provided a distraction and despite my feelings of being an outsider, I continued going. Spiky and his massive planet eyes made going to church easy and gave me something to look forward to.

My friend Sam's parents had money and a nice home. Her dad bought her a new red sports car at sixteen. When dropping me off at my house, she refused to stop her car because my neighborhood was bad. She would come to a slow crawl and force me to hop out. I got used to having friends feel afraid around mom. I felt if *those* things would have happened with Spiky, that would have wounded me badly. I couldn't take the risk of him seeing my very damaged world because to me it was no joke. I couldn't take that risk with *anyone* for that matter. I kept friends at a distance and simply didn't date. I had a few guys pursue me, but always had walls up. When people would try to come over, I would make up excuses. I would always stay at other people's homes. No one ever truly saw past the veil. No one knew the real me because I hid it.

I got invited to prom as a freshman, but I knew I had to decline. The boy, Chris, insisted on picking me up from school every morning and walked me to my first class. He even drove me home after school. Chris was one of the kindest boys, and I felt so bad pushing off his attempts to date because he truly was a caring soul. I just couldn't get involved. There was a mystery to my existence, and people had to fight to get past my walls and ultimately to get close to me. Perhaps I seemed snobbish or prudish. I definitely was *not* the low-picked fruit on the tree in that I did not give any part of myself away easily, including conversation or revealing my true feelings. My trust issues meant that I was an effort. And, when this Spiky haired boy tried to start simple conversation, I pushed him away, even though I liked him terribly. I pushed him away because my trust was annihilated at a young age, so someone having a peek into the window that was my life felt life-threatening. I held a very small amount close to myself to keep me safe from judgment. It was a *thin* curtain that could expose my reality at any moment.

There were a few interactions with Spiky. One time, when I was fourteen, a few of our friends went to a music concert. We were three rows from the stage. Spiky sat next to me. I was dancing and singing along as he watched me dance. I was oblivious to this, but my friends told me later how wide his eyes were watching me. My friends were certain that a relationship was inevitable. In my experience older boys dated freshman as a means of getting sex. I suppose younger girls are more impressionable, but Spiky wasn't like this. He was as clean-cut as they come and was clearly a good person. He seemed like the kind of guy who grew up in a Christian utopia who never experienced the dark side of life.

We would occasionally hang out at various places. One time, a few of us went to a restaurant. He sat near me and I felt his eyes on me. He gave me generously his eyes and some of his conversations. It was like he was the black hole and *I* was the stream of subatomic particles swirling around him. I couldn't help but get sucked into his orbit. My trust issues kept my guard up but inside, he already had my heart. I remained silent while around him while clinging to my friend. Another time, he drove me home, this time to my father's house. (I lived in between relatives' homes frequently because of mom's condition.) It was a poor neighborhood and an exceptionally small house. In my fifteen-year-old mind, I felt embarrassed about the home. Christians always came off as so perfect and I never fit in with that. I insisted he drop me from the street because our driveway was very badly paved. Determined to get in the driveway, he nearly ripped the bottom of his car, as he forced his way up. He watched me walk inside. Every step was a cringe moment in my soul. I thought, if only he had seen my *true* home on the eastside. This small house was *nice* compared to my real one, but still embarrassing because I knew he lived better than I did.

My teenage mind didn't feel Spiky would get it. I couldn't be the perfect Christian he had been used to. I definitely overthought it, but I didn't feel he would be able to love me past the mess. I came disassembled. I was a fixer-upper and the contractor who would eventually come into my life would need to have a lot of love, to help rebuild the broken foundation of trust. It was complicated. I needed renovation in my heart and mind. I doubted Spiky wanted a project to take on. I figured he'd probably marry a simple girl who came from a church family; he would live a simple Christian life, never leaving his zip code. He'd give his 2.5 children simple names. He'd have Sunday dinners with his kind and non-dramatic family, and they would all go to church together as one big happy bunch. Every Christmas, they would take family trips. (This is what my fifteen-year-old mind imagined perfect families did.) Meanwhile, my family moments would involve trips to rehab, jail, trying to get mom admitted to the psych ward, or the cops showing up at our house. There would be no fights in his flawless world. If I stayed in Iowa, I knew my hell would *continue* and the person dating me would feel those flames heavily by proxy. That would take tremendous strength and love from my partner to endure such a toxic situation. I was the complex Rubik's cube that most people couldn't piece together. I was the Humpty dumpty who all the king's men couldn't put back together again. I was work.

I wasn't playing games with my crush by being confusing or trying to intentionally mislead him. Even though I rejected his eye contact and rejected his conversation, he was in my heart. I was afraid. I needed to know my heart was safe and I needed a lot of reassurance. I wanted to exit my world and live permanently in his Heaven, but I was out of my element, and he definitely was out of my hellish element. For this, I hated my situation even more. It made me not normal. I hated that most girls could go get exactly what they wanted, but *that situation* would pull me in directions as opposed to the desire within my heart. I felt trapped into a certain life and my only way of escape was moving away.

At the age of sixteen, I ended up getting a job at a local store where Spiky worked. At fifteen, I found a job at a fast-food place. I picked this place to work because it was within walking distance of my grandpa's house. I lived between different relatives' homes when mom's issues would flare and as I said, my hormone years made dealing with her illness brutal. The fast-food job wasn't my *first* choice; however, I knew financially, I would need to purchase a car on my own so working was essential. I put everything I owned into savings and spent nothing. Work provided a much-needed means of escape to my home life.

During this time there was another boy, James, who began stalking me. I was kind to him, and he took my kindness as if I liked him romantically. He asked me out several times and I politely declined. I would notice him driving by my house or following me to school (we did not go to the same school). He would call my house and hang up. He would show up at places where I was. This was pre-cell phone days and it escalated where I felt afraid to walk back and forth to work. I tried to walk as quickly and aggressively as possible. He started walking up and down my street several times a day. I was thinking about finding another place to work because this boy was making me feel afraid and I needed some distance. I later discovered he'd been locked up in a psych ward a few times. I always found it interesting that the broken people were drawn to me and I suppose that was the message I was sending out to the universe. "If you have your life together, we don't fit."

Messed up people were familiar and felt comfortable to me at the time.

During a conversation at church, Spiky encouraged me to apply at his work saying, "They are hiring, you should come. It's stressful at first, but it gets better, I promise." I was only fifteen at the time so I had to wait until my sixteenth birthday before I could work at this store, but I was glad to get away. Of course, Spiky was a motivation for me to work there, but it also was within walking distance.

I was excited to work with my crush, but also kept my feelings under control.

I started the job and finished the training. I started behind the cashier's counter and eventually, I was allowed to work on the floor. I would organize products on the shelves for hours. It was boring, but it was quiet, so I didn't mind. Not long after I started the job, a girl with short hair approached me saying, "See that boy over there?" Her hair reminded me of a duck's butt in that it fluffed feather-like in the back. A popular singer at the time was Robyn, and the girl's haircut was similar. She was painfully thin and sported a bit of an RBF (resting bitch face). Her nose was beaklike; she was gaunt and boney. She quietly pointed at Spiky while keeping her back to him. He stocked shelves across the aisle from us, occasionally looking in our direction. I picked up on the fact quickly, that she was a blatantly flirty girl. She threw herself at him in a desperate and pathetic way that I found pitiful. Part of me was old fashioned and believed guys were the hunters and girls were the prey. I never saw myself as pursuing a guy, so her overtures annoyed me. I responded to RBF, "Him?" I pointed directly at him. She slapped my hand, embarrassed at my pointing, and went on to say, "He's mine and you can't like him." She had a slight condescension and bossy perk in her tone. She stated this as a territorial command locking eyes with mine. She watched me carefully for any evidence to surface that I liked "her man". By this point, I was used to lying, so I didn't give her any evidence of my crush. She stared into my eyes, frankly asking me, "Do you like him?" I paused and shook my head no. Besides, she seemed too mean to carry my secret. She could use it against me to embarrass me and I wanted to stay off the radar because I needed the money. I had no idea if he liked her in the *slightest*, but it was apparent that she was insecure. She essentially made me promise that I wouldn't intrude on the boy who was her crush. She went on to tell me, "He works in the back of the store. Only *I* can work this back end." She thought that by being close to him in proximity, that he would *want* her more. I saw several flaws in her logic, but rolled my eyes and responded, "Fine". Then with that, she walked away. It was an odd conversation. The fact that he had other girls so interested in him, along with *my* baggage, I complied with her stupid request. Her desperation and personality annoyed me, and I avoided her.

When RBF wasn't working, I, of course, worked the back end just to be able to catch a glimpse. He would be in the same aisle organizing on his side and seeing him would be a highlight in my day.

There was another boy at the store, Jake, who went around telling people we were together, which was not true. That frustrated me because I didn't want Spiky thinking I was with Jake, but at the time, I was not a confrontational person. Jake wore glasses and spit a lot when he spoke. He had a thing for me, but I wasn't interested. He pursued me and even recruited his mother into pressuring me to go out with him. It was weird but I held my ground and firmly said no. I tried to keep my nose down. I had still not dated at all up until this point.

I kept to myself and stayed quiet for the most part. I was a hard worker and stuck to working versus making friends. My goal was to save my money so I could leave Iowa. My crush and I sometimes crossed paths and we would have small chat. Early on, it seemed that Spiky was pleased he and I were working together. I felt he was analyzing me just as much as I was analyzing him. Every time he would try to talk to me or give eye contact, I would find ways to push him away because of my overthinking. He approached me at the cashier counter where he unloaded ammunition out of a returned gun. I was both startled and impressed with his ease of handling a .22. He started small chat while I mostly stood silent, wiping the counters, and listening. Even back then, I was a perfectionist and would clean the keyboard with a paperclip and bring bleach to wipe the counters. I had always associated a messy house with a messy mind, a belief brought on by my hoarding mother. He mentioned hunting and someone accidentally being shot on a recent trip. "He died," he said. "He was just a kid. It happens, you know? People get shot." he said way too casually. Until then, I almost mentioned going hunting with him, or going on a hike. However, that conversation scared me off. I wondered if Spiky was with the boy when he was killed. I wondered who shot the boy. My frightened thoughts kept me quiet. With a shocked expression, I listened and nodded. I felt a torn feeling inside because I would hope for that connection to continue, even though I knew it probably felt one-sided. I was making him work too hard. I would hope my courage would somehow surface. I would hope he would think my fruit was worth the extra effort and climb higher. Again, torn. I also felt he wouldn't understand, so I suppose I gave him mixed messages. I suppose he felt I wasn't interested which wasn't true.

One time, he grabbed me while I was working and locked eyes with mine. I think it was the cold that got him so invigorated. He had just finished putting carts away. He asked me about how things were going with the job. To me, his eyes were laser intense, shooting a hole in my face, and his very brief skin on skin contact touching my arm sent me into anxiety mode on the inside. It was impossible to keep calm on the outside. My cover of coolness was going to be blown badly if he touched me again. As mentioned, when he would look at me, I felt *seen* which made me uncomfortable because I was a hidden person. At that moment, the doubt and panic rushed in as did all the blood in my face. Because of the intensity of his stare coupled with his touch, I blurted out, lying, "I like another boy." I practically shouted it. I had to catch my breath and blinked rapidly, shocking even myself with my outburst. I regretted the statement the moment it came out of my mouth. I sensed the hurt in his expression and I myself felt horrified by the words coming out of my mouth. What was I saying? On autopilot, I went on to describe my crush on this thin, emo boy with black hair. I picked him because he happened to walk by. I had never seen this boy and couldn't tell you his name. The fictional crush was nonexistent. I made it up in that panicked moment. My words were opposite to what I felt. Did he know I was lying? Did he know how much I liked him or how afraid I felt? Could he hear my heart pounding outside my chest all because he brushed my skin? Did he see the red in my cheeks? I felt so scared like if he kept looking at me that way, he would know all my secrets. I was completely panicked. He had these eyes that made me feel like he knew my every thought and I wasn't ready to be seen. I knew if he lifted the rock that was my life, that it would uncover all kinds of ugly bugs. Truthfully, my overthinking brain couldn't see how it would work and I definitely did a lot of thinking about the situation at the time. It had such regret and I beat myself up over it for days. Part of me wondered if he was going to ask me out that day before I messed things up.

The fear got the better of me in the end. After that, I believe Spiky took my words as the truth about the emo boy and decided to stop pursuing me. He distanced himself and was no longer friendly. He no longer gave eye contact or smiled. We no longer talked, and he was cold and aloof. He seemed to be distant. He began hanging out with another girl and avoided me. That was that - he was done fishing in my pond because nothing was biting. I struggled silently with his avoidance and felt mad at myself and a little irritated at him for not understanding the complicated puzzle that was me. Throw the lure one more time, I thought. Like he should know the war going on inside my head and see the hidden secrets of my heart. I felt like Smeagol from Lord of the Rings, in that I got into my own head sabotaging my chance for a potential happy ending. Fear won. I'll never know the full truth about Spiky, or his intentions because I did not lower my guard, nor did I take the chance. I never told him how I felt. I never allowed the vulnerability of my heart, conversation, or emotions to open fully and it was a regret for some time.

He ended up asking my quirky weird friend Sam out on a date. I'm not sure if this was to get a rouse out of me, but that was how I took it. Sam was odd and boys never went for her. She dressed weird, had an odd taste in music, and had a dorky way about her. Honestly, my friend was confused. She said the date was awkward. I was baffled but I completely understood. From his position, I showed disinterest. Perhaps I hurt his ego or made things too hard. Perhaps he thought I was playing games, was confused, or was simply too damaged. I don't know. Of course, avoidance and distance were *lies* to my true feelings for him. After that, Sam asked me not to pursue him, even though she was fully convinced he had a thing for me and took her on a date to mess with my head. At that, I let my crush go. I still harbored a secret liking for a while, but always maintained a distance until I met my future husband. I no longer went to the church because of my feelings for him. I didn't allow him a chance. I let the fear win. I look back at my old sixteen-year-old self and feel sad at the issues that weighted me down.

I know now that I was incredible and amazing even then; I just couldn't see past the pain of the dysfunction surrounding my life. I wasn't living out the beauty of my potential because this situation trapped me and worse, I *let it* trap me. At the time, I didn't know that. Worse was that it wasn't really *my* dysfunction. I didn't own it, I didn't create it, I was born into it and I carried it around like a designer bag. Somehow, it defined me. That dysfunction set the path of my life in a certain direction. Had I not had such a horrible home life, perhaps I would have never left Iowa. Perhaps, I would have lived a different life entirely. At sixteen, I saw this in a negative light, like why couldn't my life be more simple? However, I no longer see it as a curse. Much of my life transpired *because* of the events of my childhood. It really shaped me into who I have become: resilient, brave, and compassionate. It made me better and things *would* get better one day, but the ending with Spiky was tough for me.

As for my thoughts about Spiky today – that was 25 years ago. Today, he and I live 1,600 miles apart. I know nothing about him and haven't seen him since I was seventeen. My life was just beginning with my future husband. The last time I saw him, we ran into one another at McDonald's just before I left town. It had been raining and there had been tornadoes that summer. The storm outside matched my inside emotions and feelings about seeing him that day. That small reminder of him brought a sadness, because of all the issues that weighed down my soul during the time he lived in my heart. My future husband had his hands groping me while I felt that Spiky watched us with a measured expression. I ordered fries and had a bad UTI at the time, which kept me running to the restroom constantly. He was sitting near the restroom. We didn't speak but his eyes were talking loudly. At that moment, I can only assume Spiky was surprised to see the prude that was me, was sexually active.

A friend later told me he did marry a simple girl and she was born into a good family and they did go on to have two kids. He lived in his same childhood zip code. I was happy for him that he found a wife who matched his uncomplicated upbringing. I found my hero in my future husband, and he was a safe place to land. His depth and deep compassion helped me to move forward. He took on a project in marrying me, that's for sure. It literally took one lure for the next guy to pull me in. He was what I needed at the time.

At seventeen, I was no longer tied to the possibility of remaining in Iowa. My future became clearer from that moment on. The dream of being with Spiky ended and my crush had left. My life consisted of being a mother to my sibling, dreaming about leaving, working, saving every penny, going to school, and mom going in and out of mental hospitals. She saw eight doctors by the time I was seventeen. I was a full-time mom to my sibling. I dressed her, fed her, did homework, picked her up from school, and dropped her off. For me, I was counting down to my exodus.

CHAPTER 19 - HIM

I had just turned seventeen when I met Him. There was a boy who was always in the backdrop of my life. I'll call him Eyebrows. We went to preschool together, shared the same babysitter, and sat in homeroom together in 7th grade. I was drawn toward him magnetically because he was quiet and distant like me. I figured that also, like me, he probably came with an interesting back story. He was a puzzle just like I was. I enjoy depth because I have experienced both height and depth in my life and complex people intrigue me. It seems that all the truly interesting people in life, have a story.

I had a few encounters with this boy. We went to preschool together. We both had the same teacher Miss Gin and there were pictures of us together as preschoolers with our graduation robes. At graduation, we ran around the park together, playing. We sat next to each other at a picnic table to eat and years later would be surprised at how many times we bumped into each other throughout our lives. We shared a homeroom class in 7th grade. I remember he dressed in black. He remembered me playing the piano and I remembered his shaggy hair that hung into his eyes. I wanted badly to take the scissors and cut his bangs. I remember another time, seeing him at Hull Avenue Park in Des Moines with some friends. I was thirteen. I was walking up the hill toward the park, while he was walking down the hill and leaving. The park was also a great place to go sledding. That day, the sun was in my eyes and I saw him from a distance and immediately felt an intense electric

pull toward him. A shot of electricity ran through my body

and I remembered thinking at that moment that I would

marry that man someday. I remember the shape of his

silhouette standing on the top of the hill of that park.

During high school, I had a friend say that she wanted to

introduce me to Eyebrows because she thought we would

hit it off. He was my type: geeky, large nose, big eyes, big

eyebrows, smart, shy, and awkward.

It wasn't long after Spiky left and stopped working

at the store that Eyebrows started. It was my junior year in

high school, and I had just turned seventeen. When Spiky

left, it felt less awkward for me because I could be free

from his attractive face and that silly notion of being with

him. This new boy moved into town from Nevada. For the

first time, I noticed Eyebrows. His eyes were so dark, they

were nearly black. I loved this. I observed everywhere I

went, he went. If I took a break, he took a break. If I

worked in a certain part of the store, he stocked the same part of the store. If I walked out to my car, he would be behind me walking out to his car. Our hours seemed to match exactly. He had very large eyebrows, dark brown eyes, and a complete mystery about him, which I loved.

An acquaintance Sammy asked me while stocking shelves at work, "Who do you like?" Quietly, I did pine for Spiky (still) but due to my internal conflict, our varying lives, his avoidance, and work departure, I simply wouldn't act on those feelings. The moment left. I liked this other boy with big brown eyes and large eyebrows that seemed to follow me around like a puppy dog. He had just started. When I mentioned Eyebrows to Sammy, her eyes grew in size and she immediately went to call him. She told me he came to her pool party and she knew him. She said that he was very funny, and she thought he liked me also based on her observation.

Eyebrows showed up after my shift ended that night. It was 10 pm and he pulled up in a red Camaro. Four cars were parked while we stood in the parking lot talking. I liked his mystery and eyes. His almost black eyes looked as if he were up to no good, but those puppy dog eyes conveyed innocence and sweetness. He possessed the look of innocence and bad boy all in one. He wore all black, with black trench boots, and had hair that hung in his face. The sexual attraction was intense and immediate between us. His allure drew me in.

That night, we stood under the stars with a few friends, including Sammy and talked. RBF with the fluffy duck-hair was there, flirting very heavily with Eyebrows, but I loved how he shot her down very directly and more than once. I thought, finally, someone else sees how annoying she is! She left after his rebuttals, while we stayed. Because of his nerves, he said some off-putting things. He mentioned that he would never have a family and that his car would always come first before his wife. He spoke about being an underwear model and also not believing in God. He basically struck out multiple times. I later found he was attempting sarcasm but failed in this moment miserably. I made him nervous. Not understanding this at the time, I felt really let down that night. As I drove home, I decided I would definitely *not* go out with this boy. I called my friend telling her what a disaster it was, and we laughed about it.

The next day, he showed up at our work and it was his day off. This time, he had on a nice buttoned-up shirt. His hair was slick back and he had a warm smile on his face. His eyes were the most incredible thing about him physically, but I liked his smile. His eyes were surrounded in these large eyebrows that brought out his Italian looks and as I said, they were very puppy-doggish. This was the first time, I noticed his smile, however. He waited for me to go to break and then asked if I would consider going on a date with him. He was so polished, kind, and nice that I thought – maybe I misjudged him last night. Arrogant and rude boys thoroughly appalled me. Two pet peeves of mine at the time were rude and ignorant people. Intellect has always been an attractive quality. I turned down rude types and forced a standard of kindness in the person I would date. I was picky.

The next night was a Friday and I agreed to go out on a date with Eyebrows. I had many doubts and almost let my overthinking brain cancel on him but decided to take a leap of faith. It was a marginal decision in my mind, but somehow, I leaned on the side of belief. Although I had some awkward encounters with boys, this was my real first official date at seventeen. I had never known love at that point. It was going to take months of effort before Eyebrows had my *full* trust, but I knew the potential of this date. It was the *first* time I considered opening myself to another person in showing my heart. I hoped he would not judge my situation. I was stepping out and ready to be seen. I was very scared but also excited.

That night in 1997, we went to a mini-golf and go-cart park. It was a warm summer night in June and the sky was clear. I wore a blue mini-skirt with a blue top and he wore a Dallas Cowboys football jersey. The smell of his car was both vanilla and leather and I remember barely being able to see over the dashboard. His interior was red and black, and he told me that his car door would sometimes fly open randomly, so I gripped his center console with white knuckles. The radio played softly a song "Glycerin" by Bush who was a popular band at the time. (Nirvana, Bush, and Stone Temple Pilots were popular bands in the late '90s.)

The entire date, he was so polite and such a gentleman. That was what I *wanted*, was a kind, gentle, and considerate guy. He knocked at my door and held my hand on the way to the car. He opened the car door for me and asked what I wanted to play on the radio. He drove carefully. Gentleness, compassion, and understanding were very important qualities to me. I wanted to avoid the pitfalls of abuse that plagued my mother and steered clear of angry and condescending types. I analyzed and noticed every detail and he was acing this date.

We ended up having a fun night at mini golf. We played a round and he won the game. He was a competitive person and also confident. I quickly learned that he was a very sarcastic person who loved puns. I *loved* his wit and he made me laugh with his dry humor. Our personalities synched easily and effortlessly. I am a perfectionistic, analytical, introvert and who has some outgoing tendencies and he is a serious, stable, intellectual, and careful personality with the driest humor possible. We fit well together. He also liked the outdoors (not as much as me) and talked about visiting places where we could hike, see the stars, camp, and jump off cliffs together. All of this sounded wonderful to me. I loved outdoor activities and dreamed of the mountains. Nature was therapeutic and something I was very drawn to. My next step in life was going to be an adventure and he was down.

The next day was a Saturday; we went to an amusement park. That day in June was hot. He held my hand and asked what I wanted to ride first. He considered me in everything and treated me with the utmost respect. I noticed he not only dressed up for me, but he also paid for every date and he opened every door. My grandfather once told me that a man should iron his clothes, comb his hair, and shave, as a form of respect toward the woman he pursues. He was born in the early 19th century and wore nice clothes every day. Grandpa always made an effort in his appearance because to dress sloppy, meant a man didn't care about himself or the woman he was pursuing. I had some old-fashioned ideas about men and Eyebrows fit perfectly. He wasn't like other boys our age; he was mature, polite, and respectful. He opened doors, he brought flowers, he walked me to my door, and he never forced anything with me.

He made me feel special, desired, and attractive. He told me how beautiful I was. This was not something I heard from a boy before. He told me how my eyes were the color of the sky and he loved my soft skin. At the amusement park, he won me a stuffed toy. We rode the buccaneer ride together and a few roller coasters. It was a lot of fun. We ate pizza for lunch. A lady threw up in front of us on the ski lift while we shouted down to people walking, "Watch out!" We rode the water ride and I had to sit on his lap. It was very awkward, but he was so kind and gentle about it, that it put my nerves at ease. I did not believe in being overly flirty with boys. He told me that I was light on his lap, so I relaxed as the water splashed us in the face and we broke out in laughter. During the Silly Silo ride, I accidentally bared my underwear to the world. It was mortifying. I wore a skirt and the spinning barrel ride has a floor that drops. My body began to slightly slip downward as my clothes stayed up. Basically, my skirt was up to my *waist* and my white laced panties were showing. I had a lot of eyes on me, but Eyebrows was a total gentleman about it and turned his eyes away, which impressed me even more. Most guys would try to sneak a peek or say a crude remark; however, his reply was kindness, which made me fall in love with him even more. He was such a good person on the *inside* and that made me love him quickly. He had quality character, morals, he was kind, and a solid person, plus he was funny. I was so drawn to the person he was inside.

He took me to his homecoming dance. We decided to double date. I wore a blue dress and pinned my blonde hair atop my head. He picked me up and held my hand, offering me his jacket. It was a cold September night and I could tell that he wanted to take care of me. The very first song we danced to was an Eric Clapton song, *Wonderful Tonight*. He held me a bit too tightly, out of nervousness, so that my breath was taken but I thought his nervousness was adorable. By the third date, I knew we were serious, and I knew he was the one. It was his character, gentle way, and old-fashioned manners which won my heart. I didn't love him for what he could do for me, but rather for who he was. He was an incredible soul.

Because his heart was so kind and he had a gentle way about him, I felt *free* opening up to him. I eventually, began telling him small pieces about my life and of my dream to move away one day and escape this place. I let him in and took off all my armor piece by piece. I took a chance and opened my heart and gave him my trust. He never broke it. He listened so well. This was the first person I'd ever told about my life and he received it and held it in such a kind way. His disarming nature meant the world to me.

His family was large, both Irish and Italian. He had a great grandmother born in Italy and another born in Ireland. His Italian grandmother was an amazing cook and both hilarious and brutally tough. His Irish family had some fighting tendencies but were all close(ish). They tended to settle things quickly with their fists then everyone would be back to getting along. Eyebrows was handsome and was my type so this was a perfect match physically. None of his family went to church but Eyebrows was open to going with me. His mother *loved* being a mom. She was a homemaker, an excellent cook, and loved ceramics and baking. She was all about her family. Being mostly Irish, she loved everything Irish. She loved the dancers, the Celtic music, the accents, and even the fashion. Her dream has always been to go to Ireland one day, however she jokes that she never will because of her fear of flying over the ocean. Later, she and I would become very close, but it wouldn't be an easy road because of my baggage. When you are guarded, I think it's natural for people to question why, as if you are hiding something. It took time for me to fully open to his family. His dad was a quiet man, much like his son. He worked very hard and loved his family. He was peaceful and reserved and never lost his temper or was provoking. There was nothing his father wouldn't do for his children and I respected him hugely for his stability and never witnessed such a stellar father figure, outside of my grandpa. Papa is dad to me now and I love him very much. He is one of the greats in my life.

Eyebrows explained that he lived in Iowa by himself, with his own apartment and set-up, while his family lived in Nevada. He was a junior in high school, but extremely independent. I loved that about him. By this point, I had about $3,000 saved up to move with no solid plan. My pre-boyfriend plan was to head east. I was going to find a job and take night classes. I would be doing it alone, but it would be an adventure and I wasn't afraid to go by myself. I think one thing about having non-parents is that it teaches you independence. I never relied on anyone and became very self-sufficient. I didn't see myself as a weak female but felt I could do anything and without support. Perhaps it was a little naïve, but I was fearless in that regard.

It was early in our relationship, but our feelings developed quickly. We spent every day together. Mom didn't like him, but that was further vindication that he was a truly good person. She seemed to like the bad ones and had *horrible* taste in men. She would find the most insane person in the room and hook up with them.

I fell in love with the man he was and handed him my heart. He was more to me than eye candy; he was soul food. He loved and nourished my soul. He was more to me than his beautiful black eyes and large eyebrows. His heart was lovely. We connected physically, conversationally, affectionately, intellectually, spiritually, and eventually sexually. He fed every part of my being and his humor was perfection. He felt safe, like a warm coat, made just for me.

By the third date, I felt a deep connection with him. I loved that he could be trusted with this heavy weight and secret that had plagued my life. My family secrets weighted my soul down and he allowed me to take off the heavy armor. My past didn't change his opinion of me. If anything, he respected me more for having gone through all that at such a young age. He said that externally, he didn't know how I was as strong as I was. I loved seeing myself the way he saw me because he saw me as this exceptionally beautiful soul. He has always thought very highly of me and continues to show me a love in myself, that I never knew existed. He is wonderful at loving, which I credit his parents for. He's a good lover and a fierce protector. He loves me the way I should've been loved all those years. To this day, I have never met anyone who loves me the way he does.

We started spending every day together. Our force was magnetic. He was patient and took things very slowly with me all the while doing and saying all the right things. It did feel picture-perfect. There were no issues and we synched perfectly together.

Six months into the relationship, we shared our very first kiss. Friends joked with us about taking so long to kiss, but mostly it was my issues that caused such a delay. He was not the kind of person to ever force me into anything I wasn't ready for. Once we started kissing, we never stopped. Kissing each other and cuddling made the connection between us grow even stronger. My love language is affection and hugely words of affirmation, so I tend to love praise. His love language is quality time; as we both deposited our love into each other's banks, our connection grew. His smell was intoxicating. He smelled like wood, soap, and peppermint. I couldn't get enough of his presence. We spent nearly every day together.

His first experience in seeing mom's illness up close was the night that she brought a stranger home for casual sex. The man had stringy black hair, wore a leather jacket, and was covered in tattoos. He appeared to be high on crack. She began provoking the stranger physically, revealing her illness on full display. It was a loud night of fighting. She tried to get Eyebrows to fight this middle-aged stranger. Eyebrows just looked at me puzzled and said to her plainly, "I'm out of your drama." At that, he turned and walked away. She chased him into the bathroom and began criticizing him. I was stunned at his ability to not be pulled into her crazy. She was taken aback as well. She tried to provoke Eyebrows further, and that's when he grabbed my hand and we left together. From that moment forward, she tried very hard to separate us because she realized she had no power over him.

His second experience in dealing with her illness was when she invited him to a free meal at a Mexican restaurant. She without warning tried to run without paying the bill and tried to get Eyebrows to participate in this crime with her. He does not break the law and is quite firm on that. Eyebrows just looked at me, completely baffled. I explained that this was normal for her and to this day, he refuses to eat publicly with her. He stood up to her and firmly drew boundaries with her. I was in awe and loved him for this.

At 6 months, we were still only kissing but knew we wanted to be together permanently. I knew he was my future. He proposed at 6 months with a diamond ring and also gave an amethyst ring and two beautiful necklaces. One was a gold heart and one was silver. He would spoil me frequently with items, to show his love and affection for me, which I was not used to, but enjoyed thoroughly. He told me constantly how beautiful I was. I felt so loved.

Around six months, we had been talking about a future together and started talking about moving to Nevada. I was warming up to the idea. I knew virtually nothing about Nevada, but it sounded like a new start to me, which I needed and craved. Plus, I *loved* the mountains and it was near several places, such as Tahoe, San Francisco, and Oregon, which fit our outdoor lifestyles. We both knew we wanted to stay active and do things outdoors such as fishing, hiking, camping, bike riding, and swimming and Nevada fit that.

Grandpa used to say that women are like a crockpot. They take a long time to get ready and become close whereas men get there more quickly, in terms of love. With every act of love, my affection and trust in him grew. As time progressed, I wanted to make love very badly, but it took me time to fully open and trust him. And, once I did trust him, he really had *all* of me. I held nothing back. I needed to know that my heart was safe with him. Every opportunity that came where he could betray me, he stayed loyal and loving. There was never any sown doubt from him, and he held my heart perfectly. That built a sense of security between us. To this day, I can talk about literally everything with him. There are no walls and no secrets with us. There is freedom in our conversation. He can be trusted to be stable which I needed desperately in my childhood. I appreciate his stability more than he'll ever know. He is loyal. He is kindhearted. He is a great person.

I had *a lot* of walls, so it took me 11 months before we became intimate. I had some bad sexual situations as a child and was told to lie about what had occurred so that took me some time before I felt I could trust a man with my naked body. With the events of Dane mutilating mom's breast when I was a small child, I was especially sensitive to being touched on my breasts. That memory was a strong flashback for me for some time, but Eyebrows was more than patient and never forced anything with me. He was always delicate.

At 11 months together, and nearly every day spent together, one night we walked hand in hand near the Des Moines River. The stars were out, and it was a clear night and the air was warm. I knew in my heart that I wanted him to have my body, heart, mind, and soul. He was already living in many of those areas already. I was about a month away from graduating high school and we were engaged. I knew I was ready. That night was the first time for both of us. I told him that I was ready to take the next step with him and gently placed his hand on my breast. He asked if I was sure and remained very patient while touching my skin softly, causing goosebumps to raise on my skin. He stroked at my cheek and I told him, yes. He gently removed my bra and I slipped off my panties, becoming completely naked in front of him. It was a feeling unlike I have ever felt. My body trembled as he touched me. I couldn't stop shaking. He slowly lowered himself onto me, kissing my cheek, lips, and forehead. He was gentle and kind, as he always is. I felt the shock of his size and nearly held my breath in pain. He took it slow for me, which seemed to torture him immensely, but he kept a slow and steady pace. It stung a lot and came with a lot of pain. I had to ask him to stop twice because I could not handle the stinging. The first time was special to me, but it was also very painful. That night something shifted in our connection and it was apparent that our hearts were deeper. This was no longer dating; it was the beginning of a lifelong relationship. There was no going back.

It took about three times of lovemaking before the stinging pain stopped. Once we made love, there was no turning back for me. He had all of me. I always enjoyed being on top and would rock my hips in small circles while

he softly caressed my breasts. The very first time I felt an

orgasm, I wasn't sure what was happening. I had never

pleasured myself. No one really had the "sex talk" with me,

even though I would see porn on the tv, and hear people

having sex. When the pleasure ripped through me, I yelled

out, "Wh—aat iii—ss thii---ss?" He looked up at me and

laughed at my innocence. All of these intimate moments

built our connection stronger together until we were a force

that could not be stopped.

We became very good at lovemaking and did it

everywhere, all the time. Once, we managed to do it 13

times in one day. I have *no* idea where we got the energy or

stamina, but we couldn't keep our hands off of each other. I

brought emotional passion and he brought a serious

intensity and together, it was powerful. We made love in

the woods, in the lake, in a hot tub, on the trampoline, in a

car, in the bathroom, and once nearly broke his parent's

bed. I was mortified to later find that his mother was home and heard our moans. It took me a long time to be able to look her in the face after that, but she thought that our love was cute. She had met her husband at the same age and went on to tell us that she was once just like us many years ago. Our love reminded her of their love. I liked that his parents were not judgmental types and they were down to earth people with no pretense about them. They weren't expecting a perfect girl, which helped me be more at ease around them.

We couldn't keep our hands off of each other. Once the door for sex opened, we wanted each other nearly every second of every day. We drove people crazy. This went on for a few years and some of our friends became very annoyed with our constant displays of affection and tendency to slip away for 30 minutes. We both had octopus' arms and constantly grinded and groped on each other. It was like the world turned off and only we existed. It felt like there was no love story like *our* love story and the

passion we had between the two of us was world changing.

His depth was intense and amazing and my emotion for

him was overwhelming. It was passion all the time.

A few times, she tried to separate us, however, it

was pointless. She banned him from the house, but he

frequently crawled in my window at night. She tried to

force a relationship between me and another person, which

didn't work. At one point, she tried to get him to leave me

for what she claimed was, "a more beautiful girl." She

brought the girl to our house and invited him over. With the

girl next to us, she began to say how this girl was so much

more beautiful than me. "Her ass is smaller," she taunted. I

was horrified at her words. They cut me and I began to cry.

He did not take the bait to her crazy and answered her by

kissing me and telling me no one was as beautiful as me

and he loved my ass. As a last resort, she recruited several

of my friends to try to convince me to leave him, including

my grandparents, best friend, another friend, and a cousin. It was pitiful. One of my friends brought a guy over to set me up. He was tall, a smoker, and very much a player. Of course, mom loved him. It was never going to happen. There was this big effort to try to get me to break things off with Eyebrows. By that point, I was in love and it was too late.

Eyebrows had such a propensity of protection that there quickly became tension between mom and him because she was a source of hurt in my life. She saw it as a power struggle, and he saw it as an act of love to protect me from someone who frequently hurt me. I loved him for this. I never felt protection prior to him. I protected myself in silence, in lies, secrets, and in hiding, but never received it from a parent.

After we were intimate, mom was in a full-blown spell. I think she knew she was going to lose me soon and tried to control everything she could. She became very

drunk one night and came onto Eyebrows sexually. There

was a big party at our place, and she was drinking beer all

night. She tried to kiss him and put her hands all over him,

trying to dance with him. He firmly told her no and

flattened his hand, forcing a distance between them. Her

drunk ego was hurt, and she came over and slapped me

across the face in rage. His parents were there, and I felt

mortified over her breakdown. I asked, "What was that

for?" "You're a whore!", she yelled. She went on to yell in

front of her friends telling them what a slut I was and of me

losing my virginity. She concocted a false story that I had

bled all over her bed. She tried to tell his parents that

Eyebrows wasn't my first. "She's going to get pregnant and

ruin his life," she told them. "Look at her... trash," she

mocked. "She's going nowhere," she said to Eyebrows. I

stood there, feeling her knife lodged in my heart, unable to

speak. She had sex all the time with strangers so why did

she have such an issue with this? Her stating my

worthlessness hurt me more than her lies claiming I had sex

with other people. She went on, "I should've gone through

with the abortion." "You were my biggest fucking

mistake." She had me locked into her hold now and I was

being verbally electrocuted by her publicly. Horrified, he

grabbed me and said "We're never coming back. You are

done hurting her," and walked away. She would later tell

people that Eyebrows had severely disrespected her that

night. That was her version of events. We had absolutely no

plan, but that night he was my knight. With tears streaming

down my face, he led me back to his car and we drove off.

That night, we slept in a tent. I fell asleep in his

arms. The future felt so uncertain, but somehow, I felt safe.

I knew that soon this would be over. Soon, I would have

real distance between her and me and that thought brought

me relief.

I loved that he rose to protect me without hesitation. I tended to not know where the line of boundaries and dignity began. It was very blurry. Abuse was blurry because I was so accustomed to it. There was an endless endurance that existed with the pain she inflicted. He helped me see that dignity line. He helped me with drawing boundaries, and I loved him for it. I couldn't wait to begin a life with this man, and he showed his incredible heart with every word, touch, kind deed, and choice. If love was a bank, he was over a million by this point. He built up my trust and showed me my heart was safe with him. He healed the pain she caused me. His love was proven by his actions. He was consistent and generous.

A month before my graduation, mom had a very bad spell. Sometimes, life events can cause this to happen. I ended up leaving home at seventeen because Eyebrows and mom got into a fight over her attacking me physically and verbally. He grabbed my hand and we never looked back.

We lived a vagabond existence off of the money we had saved. We would camp and stay in hotels. I was young and adventurous and didn't mind the ever-changing bed situation. We had each other. Anything was better than at home. One night, somehow, mom managed to steal my car in the night. I'm still not sure how she did this because I only had one set of keys. I can only assume she made a copy when I wasn't aware. I paid cash for this car and owned the title. We managed to get the car back, but it came with a lot of drama and struggle. At one point, she came to my school begging the principle to hold me back a grade. "She doesn't deserve to graduate," she pleaded. This was her way of forcing me to stay but I had one foot out the door.

The last time I saw her, she was not well. She showed up at the place we were staying, screaming, "You are coming home now!" She slammed her car door and marched toward me aggressively. It was very close to my

18th birthday and also, I was close to graduating. Her power over me was gone. I told her, "I'm leaving and there is nothing you can do about it." Rage took over her face. "Don't come crawling to me when he breaks your fucking heart." "I don't want anything to do with it." Her words were just more manipulation in trying to get me to turn to her in fear. At this point, my sibling was crying, and she wouldn't let me hug her. She stomped off in anger and that was our goodbye. It was painful. My heart ached. Leaving my sibling behind was difficult and that guilt would eat at me for many years to come, but I simply couldn't endure one more day in hell with that woman.

I graduated soon after and we left as soon as we could. Mom wouldn't let me take my things, but I didn't care. Burn it, I thought. My car was packed with blankets, food, and a tent. Our plan was to camp across the US from Iowa to Nevada. We would take our time to get there and enjoy the journey, of course making love in every state. By this point, we had lived off of some of our savings, so we didn't have as much, but just enough.

He's my best friend and he's been so much more to me than I could ever thank him for. I feel he took on a "project" in marrying me, but he's never once complained. He loved me through it all and despite it all.

CHAPTER 20 - NEVADA

When I left Iowa, it was raining. It was like the city was crying for us, not wanting us to leave but I couldn't be happier leaving!

I dreamed a thousand dreams of leaving. That was one of the happiest moments of my life. Sayonara Iowa, I waved as we drove into Nebraska, with the biggest grin spread across my face! I had no reservations and no hesitations. There were no tears. It was shouts, claps, and screams as we left.

As we drove across the country, we stopped in several places, making a vacation out of it. We stopped at the zoo in Omaha, Nebraska. We enjoyed the mountains in Utah and enjoyed a picnic and a park. In Colorado, we swam in the pool, made love, took pictures, and enjoyed our road trip along the way. In Wyoming, my car broke down. We discovered it was the engine. That was tough news as we were in the middle of our road trip, but we decided to go with it and try not to let it drag our trip down. We decided to put everything we owned into storage and made the last leg to our destination, Nevada.

When we arrived in Nevada, it was past midnight. I was surprised by the lights of the city. This was a town that didn't sleep. I was used to everything being shut down by 10 pm in Iowa. People were out on the streets, stores were open, and the town seemed alive. The air was much crisper, and it felt cleaner. There was no green at all, and the tan vegetation had a thirsty look.

We camped for a bit until it became too cold, but camping wasn't stressful. It was fun for us. This was an adventure.

We got our first place which was incredibly modest. Ok, it was a dump. But we kept a sense of humor about it. I came from nothing, so anything was better than that. I saw it all through the lens of optimism. It was a very small studio. There was no shower curtain or bedspread. The landlady smelled very badly and when we would pay rent, as we approached her apartment, the smell would be outside. Eyebrows would hold his breath as he paid rent. Our car was this tore-up brown piece of junk and we preferred to walk places rather than drive that thing. We nicknamed it the "honey wagon". It only got up to 45mph and the former driver was a chain smoker so everywhere you touched in the car, there was a sticky tar residue. Our first place was a small studio that was only $400 a month. Someone had been murdered two doors down, so it wasn't the safest, but honestly, I felt so ecstatic to start this new life with my love. As we looked out the window, there was a gorgeous view of the snowcapped mountains so every morning, I would look up and feel thankful for the view and of this new chapter in my life. This shack was better than the crazy I was so accustomed to. Honestly, it was peaceful without mom's crazy. I almost didn't know what to do not having a constant crisis. I was so on alert all the time, that not having a crisis felt unusual.

I knew virtually nothing about being a wife. I had no real example of what wives did. Eyebrows patiently ate my hotdogs and my crunchy mac n' cheese without complaint. Sometimes for dinner, we would have pretzels! I laugh now, but I had *no* clue how to cook or be a wife. I had some truly hilarious cooking stories in those early days. Once, I tried to make noodles but realized that instead of flour, I had used powdered sugar. It turned into a paste that was impossible to remove from the utensils. We ended up throwing the spoon away and the bowl. It was a disaster. Another time, I was so proud to cook my first meal in the oven and watched as he picked long hairs out of his teeth. Later, I made chocolate chip cookies and it simply had a one in front of the ingredients. The page was torn so I assumed it was one full cup of baking soda. Those were some very bitter and sour tasting cookies. For his first upside-down pineapple cake, I forgot to put in the oil, so it was quite sticky, and stuck to the roof of our mouths, but still tasted decent. I think the worst was when I tried to bake a turkey but left everything inside the turkey, including the plastic. The neighborhood cats wouldn't even eat that turkey! His mother had been such an amazing cook. I had a lot to live up to and zero skills to match her. But I was good at love and we made love constantly. It was multiple times a day, loud, everywhere, powerful, soft, tender, and lustful. Those early days, we easily did it 4-5 times a day. The sexual and emotional connection was always very strong between us despite my horrible cooking skills. He had a lot of depth, so we shared incredible conversation. We also connected on a comedic and spiritual level. I tried to not take things so seriously because this was an adventure after all. It was never going to be perfect. Finding humor was essential.

We started from zero, or arguably negative. We had nothing: no furniture, silverware, bed, plates, or sheets. We had no towels, tables, lamps, or hangers. We literally had lawn chairs in our living room for a time until someone donated a couch to us. The couch had large wires poking out and when you went to sit, your stomach dropped because the couch was so low to the ground. We were poor but it was an adventure. We made life fun. We were in love. We were figuring out life together and the monsters were all behind me. This was our life that we were building. It was all new even if it was a humble beginning.

After our first place, we got into a two-bedroom apartment with an upstairs view. We lived near a Chinese restaurant and would smell the food every night. Eyebrows had a thing for Chinese food after I turned him onto cashew chicken, and we spent *so* much money at that Chinese restaurant across from our apartment.

We would have to walk around the balcony to see the mountain view, but I loved that view. Our neighbors were from Louisiana and were always inviting us over for Cajun gumbo and crawfish. Our other neighbor was from Oklahoma and she began giving me cooking lessons, after I once horribly burned fried potatoes, setting off the smoke alarm. Our apartment turned to smoke from the burned food which ended up ruining the pan. Eyebrows joked with me about how not everything needed to go on level 8 on the stove.

The very first television we got was found at a thrift store and the only channel we received was a religious channel that featured televangelists Paul and Jan Crouch. Eyebrows made me laugh for hours as he talked about potential ways that Jan's wig had been so huge. His funniest joke was when he said a basketball had been cut in half and a wig had been glued onto the basketball and placed atop her head. Another time, I told him that I missed my exercise videos and he came out with these horrendous tight biker shorts with dumbbells, doing an exercise routine in front of me. It was hilarious. He was trying to get me to participate and laid on his back, kicking his toes. I laughed until I couldn't breathe. We found our own entertainment. Of course, we had no air conditioning in those days so we would lay on our bed for hours with frozen peas draped across our forehead and torso. He would joke, "Baby, one day we will laugh at this." Thank God we had a sense of humor.

In those early days when we were living paycheck to paycheck, Eyebrows asked me to help shave his neck one time. The clippers jumped out from my hands and took an entire section of hair out of his head. I said, "Oh no." He said, "Oh god, what did you do woman?" He saw the large bald patch saying, "Well, that's the last time you will cut my hair." We laughed. From then on, he loved having a shaved head! Silver lining.

One time in the apartment, we had this very strong odor and there were gnats everywhere. We searched high and low and could not find the source of the smell. After several days, we discovered it was that meat (beef of some sort) I tried to cook. Apparently, I left it in the oven and completely forgot about it. It had been months! We teased each other over who was going to take it out of the oven. It was pure comedy. I had so much to learn but he was never mean about my lack of skills. He kept a sense of humor.

Another time I had a bottle soaked on the counter, with a hint of dish soap. He thought it was water and began to chug it, only to discover it tasted like dawn dish soap. After that, he bought me a dish rack.

Understandably, his mother was worried about him marrying such an incapable cook. She frequently brought us meals, which I am so thankful for. Because of her, I have a few sensational gourmet hit-wonder meals and I can cook. She's given me a few cooking lessons and even created a cookbook for me.

Our very first Christmas tree was just the top of a fake Christmas tree, so it stood about one foot from the ground. It had 3 bulbs on it! The good part was putting

Christmas away took all of five minutes. We had humble

beginnings.

Two years to the date from our very first date, we

married in a small ceremony by the beach in Tahoe. It was

small, beautiful, intimate, and us. As mom walked me

down the aisle, she whispered in my ear in a low tone,

"You want to run baby girl? Just say the word...." I just

laughed. It was so like her to say something so crazy.

During the ceremony, the preacher hocked a loogy and we

just looked at each other. Yep, this is our life. Then at the

end, the photographer handed us our film and said very

rudely, "I want my tip now!" Both my parents got into a

fight. It was both sad and hilarious. Someone stole gifts

from us and at one point, I lost my wallet. We tried to not

take it all so seriously. We were in love and that was all

that mattered. Life wasn't perfect, obviously and having a

sense of humor got us through those moments. That is how

we deal with my crazy family even to this day, is with

humor. (By the way, Eyebrows does a sensational impression of mom). Our honeymoon was typical us in that we went camping in the mountains and then drove to the ocean. We love the outdoors and hike and fish often. We did a backpack hike in the mountains and came across a bear. He joked with me because I drank out of a waterfall and he was concerned I would get giardia, but Tahoe had the cleanest water I'd ever drunk in my life! To this day, when we hike to the waterfall, I bring canteens of water back to drink.

I never looked back at that hell. The memories are sometimes painful, but that is over.

Years later, it's been nearly a quarter of a century that we've been married. It's been two solid decades with this man who holds my heart so carefully. I didn't come with a lot to give, and he showed me, love. He showed me connection, freedom, and trust. He showed me, family. He showed me stability. He definitely showed me patience with my cooking! We have traveled the US together, traveled abroad, finished college, and had a child. I had no idea this boy would get in my head, my heart and end up changing everything. He not only changed the course of my life, but he changed who I was and how I *saw* myself. Under his love, my self-esteem began to soar to new heights. That's what loving someone will do. It makes them rise. He brought a sense of security I didn't know existed. He holds my secrets and keeps the vulnerable areas protected. I can trust him with my heart and my life. He's truly a partner.

Everything that we have built over the past 24 years has been a journey. I won't pretend that it has been a perfect ride, especially for him, in dealing with some of the baggage my past has brought. He definitely can flash the crazy in-law badge and I'm certain I've caused a few of those white hairs on his beard. Everything I've learned has been learned via trial and error experience. That was true for cooking, being a wife, cleaning, and pretty much every other area in my life. I had *no* example of marriage, health, parenting, finances, or even doing relationships or communication healthily. It was a bumpy road because I had to learn all those things with my partner and on my own. I'll say it again - I'm glad he had a sense of humor.

Eyebrows taught me a lot about what it is to have a good marriage, what good communication is, how to have balance and health in your life. He gives me the right amount of love and freedom. He likes to watch me go for my dream and supports me in my choices. He loves me. He's never insecure to see me rise as high as I can. He is an incredible father. He never shuts down my feelings, as my father did. I am in awe of his parenting skills. I've never witnessed anything like his example as a father. He is so patient, gentle, loving, and kind to our daughter. Everything he teaches her is through that base of kindness and respect.

266

I grew up with violence, so to see that example done a completely different way, is inspiring. He's been a teacher to me. Humiliation, torture, and abuse were tools used to control me as a child and I watch our daughter bloom with none of those horrible traits existing. She doesn't live in fear and has never once had a panic attack in her life. She goes for what she wants, and we support her wholeheartedly. She communicates how she feels and has so much more confidence than I did her age. I am satisfied she will never experience a life of suffering, as that line has ended with me and she knows a different life entirely.

When I became a parent, that changed everything for me. We waited fifteen years before we had a child and we did that on purpose. I wanted to wait until I felt I had something substantial to offer a child and also make sure that my issues had been somewhat resolved. I literally started at ground zero. I was determined to not put any of my baggage onto my child. Having our daughter was the best day of our lives. It was a surprise to me how she sparked childhood memories and caused them to come to the surface. I actually grieved for a time after we had her because when I would see her doing anything like riding a bike, swimming, or bathing, I would have flashbacks of myself as a young girl. A lot of memories came up after she was born that I had buried. I couldn't comprehend or wrap my head around the horrendous suffering I had endured, after now having met my daughter. I never knew a love so strong as the love I had for this child. I began to show myself real compassion, for the first time.

CHAPTER 21 – A NEW LIFE

When our daughter was born, my mom and father were not present, but Eyebrow's family all came. They showed enough love that we barely noticed anyone missing. It was a 19-hour labor and her head was quite large. We tease her about being smarter than all the other kids because of her large brain. I knew she would be happy because I felt extremely happy the entire pregnancy even though it felt I was toting a bowling ball on my pelvis. Since the day she was born, she was persnickety. Literally on day one, she demanded I breastfeed her only one way. She preferred the right side only. At three we found her bossing the other kids on the playground, and the first day of kindergarten she literally took off running as soon as I parked the car. "See you mom!" She has no fear. She's independent, sarcastic, logical, and hilarious just like her dad. My daughter is nearly ten now and a straight-A student who is on the honor roll. She is strong-willed, tough, a tomboy, and I feel so proud to be her mother. I love watching her assert her beautiful personality into the world. Her intelligence and sarcasm are superlative. I feel thankful for this life and the family I have. I know my story could've been very different.

It took me nine years before I visited back home to Iowa. I had mixed feelings about visiting. Mom ended up having a bad spell and I said goodbye to her from the mental hospital. She brought all the garbage up from the basement and insisted I go through all her feces-covered papers. She began throwing papers in the living room and brought out piles of junk, demanding I sort through it. She offered to sign her house over to me and begged me to stay in tears. At one point, she broke down sobbing, while we were folding socks, saying, "I wish I had you when I was a baby. I needed you as a mom," she said. She later drove all over town in a zig-zag fashion until we nearly ran out of gas. It was a chaotic mess of erratic behavior. My family begged me to stay, but I was in college at the time and needed to get back for finals. It wasn't a fun trip, seeing her fall apart like that. Boarding the plane, knowing she was in a psych ward made me feel a lot of guilt.

I especially felt a tremendous amount of guilt over my sibling and the difficult life she was forced to live. I left her behind in that hell with very little support. I told myself I couldn't handle one more second of that life, and I left. What I didn't realize was that *I* was all she had. I was her mother. I tucked her into bed at night. I made her meals and dressed her for school. I made sure her homework was done. I combed her hair and held her when she was afraid. She suffered horribly when I left, and I blamed myself for her anguish and pain. She nose-dove into darkness and I felt it was my fault. She had no one to grab onto because by then my grandparents were in their 90s. Her father introduced her to drugs, she endured many abusive relationships, ran away, struggled to become clean, and nearly lost her life. I hated seeing her struggle and accepted the responsibility of that 100%. If I could have brought her with me to Nevada, I would have. I wanted to rescue her but by then she was in too deep. I couldn't pull her out. It was a fast descent. She had to experience her own landslide journey before reaching her pinnacle success and sobriety some 20 years later. It was a hard and strenuous climb for her, but she did it in her own strength and with little support. To become the person she is, she had to lose everything. Her feet touched the ocean floor of pain.

Sometimes true change comes at the cost of extreme pain; some of us cannot change until we feel so uncomfortable, we have to change. I am so proud of the woman she is.

When I come home, I always feel torn if I should tell mom I'm in town. I don't want to disrupt her health and visiting home is hard. That's why I tend to visit once every ten years. I miss Iowa and love home but my relationship with mom complicates it. Going home is usually not a fun event. Most of the memories are not happy for me in my childhood home. Being back in my family home is emotionally painful and brings memories, but Iowa will forever and always be home to me. Iowa and the memory of it are both sweet and sour.

Mom visited me out of state in Nevada. She had a very bad spell and I had just gotten out of major surgery. She did one of her many disappearing acts. She was missing for over a month. The first time the police found her, she was living by a river in northern California. She was found again a few weeks later, this time in Coos Bay, Oregon by the pacific coast. Eventually, she was picked up in southern Idaho. Every time the police found her, she would slip away again. She had rented a car, and to this day, they have never located the car or her purse for that matter. She had to get entirely new forms of ID and license after that event. She ended up being found in a desert, in the middle of literally nowhere. No one understood how she got there. She showed up at a stranger's house, who had no neighbors for miles. They were perplexed at how she got into that area and to this day, we don't know.

Once the police finally detained her, they escorted her from border to border, all the way back to Des Moines, Iowa, and eventually to the mental hospital where she could get medication, sleep, therapy, and treatment. It is not difficult to comprehend how so many mentally ill people are homeless. I am thankful that my family kept her off the streets. It was only after she was locked in, that my body was able to recover from the surgery.

I will never allow our daughter to be alone with my mother. I always knew that would be the case with her based upon many of the abuses I endured. Some may think that to be cruel, but I don't feel that my daughter would be safe considering mom's history. Once when we went home to visit, mom's house was infested with bugs and fleas and she became belligerent because we wouldn't put the baby on the floor to crawl. She tried to give her a toy that was soaked in urine. I don't feel that mom is equipped to always *know* what is best for a child. I live very far away which creates a boundary but also, I will at times decide to redraw those lines depending on how I feel her illness is impacting me and my family. My family comes first, and I cannot jeopardize my daughter's wellbeing because of my mother's illness. It is a tough situation but that is my reality. I love her enough to still be in her *life*, but there will always be a wall with us. That keeps things healthy and allows me to not get pulled into her crazy. I married someone who is great at boundaries and I am thankful for that. He tells me boundaries don't mean you don't love the person; it means you love them enough to make things healthy for both of you. He tells me that it's okay to have dignity and that when someone is hurting you, you are not expected to tolerate it endlessly. Setting limits is good for both people. That mentality is different from the one I grew up believing. I know now I cannot fix her and I need to allow her to be responsible.

Moving away not only ended up being the best decision for *me* but it became good for mom as well. It pained her but she was forced to take responsibility for her wellbeing. I am proud of who she is and how far she has come. She is doing well, and I have learned to have realistic expectations and also to tend to my own backyard. We all have our own ball of string and I stick to untangling mine for the most part. Knowing and speaking the truth about how I felt about my life was important to healing me. It honored my feelings. Mom's health matters to me but it is *hers* to manage and she is doing a beautiful job. I am proud of her.

I look back and realize that I had every opportunity to walk straight into the thralls of abuse, pain, and addiction. It was familiar. It *was* comfortable. That was the trajectory my life faced. But I saw what I lived through and wanted something else entirely. I always fought against that path. I believed a better life was *possible* and for that belief, I am thankful to God. Many people can never break free from the chains of abuse, addiction, pain, and mental illness because they don't believe there is a better way. There definitely is. It's a lot of work. That ability exists within all of us already to build and live a happier life. It's all choices and consequences.

My life today is night and day compared to the childhood I survived. We have a nice home, I finished college, we live in a beautiful state, and have a blessed life and family. We have been fortunate to travel abroad, I've spoken publicly about mental illness and my experience, and I am passionate about health as a whole, but particularly about mental health. If ever I tell people about my past, they usually cannot understand how I turned out so normal. It is hard for people to make the leap between where I came from versus where I am today. I credit my grandparents for everything. Without them, I would've been a statistic.

It has taken me years to try to gain some understanding of why I suffered so much. It has taken time to understand my true feelings, which I buried so deep in an effort to protect myself from the pain of the truth. Honestly, I had pitiful moments. I had angry moments and sad moments. That's all part of acceptance and grief. As to why

I suffered; some would say it is luck of the draw. Some would say it was *choices* which my parents made, life itself, or that mom's situation was a tragedy. Some would say there is a bigger purpose at play here and I tend to favor the latter. I want to use the pain to create something beautiful. I want to be transparent in sharing my story. Beauty and pain go hand in hand. I think of the labor pain I felt before my daughter came into my life, as she ripped eighteen stitches worth of flesh. Because of the pain of my childhood, I appreciate all the good today and I truly *savor* life.

I consider my small voice to be that of a mental health advocate. I know in reading my brutally honest story, many may feel upset over the actions of the ill person in my life. But, please don't. My love for her is unconditional. My understanding of her disease is great. Her difficulty created compassion in me, and her imperfection is perfectly her. Our story is one I want to share because mentally ill people are people too. She didn't choose to be ill. She was a victim of the disease and finding help felt impossible at the time. Mentally ill people deserve all the things we want in life: happiness, love, hope, and freedom. I have never seen the illness as being *her*. I know the real her is magnetic, heartfelt, and sensitive. I see the light that exists inside her and I know the real her. I accept her the way she is, and I don't expect her to become something different, to appease insecurity within me. I am capable of loving her as she is, even with the illness. God knew that and it's made us both stronger individuals. Imperfection *is* a gift. Sometimes love is hard. Some argue against that, saying love shouldn't be hard. But when you love a broken person, love is definitely hard. When you sit in the rooms of Alanon and hear the stories of other people dealing with their loved ones who cause pain, you understand that real love overcomes pain, but love does come at a cost.

I have become so secure with my story that I am unafraid to share it. That wasn't always the case. I once kept it a *hidden* secret but now I feel safe within myself to tell my truth. I feel that each time we bare our scars, it helps others show theirs. There's something healing in transparency and openness. In allowing people to feel your vulnerability, it opens the way for them to show theirs. We are all human and we are all imperfectly perfect.

I still go to Alanon. It's been years but I feel it still helps my life. A lot of the things they teach help me with boundaries. They help me resist the urge to be a fixer, as I personally am programmed to be. They help me define my relationships and help me to slow down and think before I react. Is this really mine to own or is it theirs? I feel attending makes my relationships healthier. It makes me aware of my own character flaws to judge or to fix, or take responsibility, so I can avoid those familiar traps. One of the most life-changing books I've ever read is called *Adult*

Children of Alcoholics. Reading that book, made me feel 100% understood for the first time in life. I know the book is speaking of alcohol, but it easily could have been written about mental illness as well. Insanity is the same. That book read me. It put on word to paper, how dysfunction impacts a child. I am the quintessential perfectionistic, super responsible, peacemaker. I tend to think anything can be fixable which is both a blessing and *something I need to be careful with.* Some buildings need to be torn down so new ones can be built just like some trees are not savable. Fixing isn't always the way. Some marriages aren't fixable and sometimes you need to know when to draw the dignity line. That book helped me to understand why I am the way I am and helped me avoid the pitfalls that come with my character defects.

It was at age thirty-four, that I went to my first ever therapy session. Therapy changed my life. I was *so* ambivalent about going. The fear of crazy kept me away. There is a huge stigmatism associated with therapy but getting help for your mind and heart is nothing to be ashamed of. I did the best I could on my own, and my therapist helped me navigate the difficult terrain of trauma. She helped me to fill in the holes my parents had left.

My advice is to be picky about your therapist. I knew that her qualities and strengths were things that she could impart to my life and so I chose her.

Therapy tapped me into the superwoman inside. I wish I would have gone at fourteen! I found there was a profound depression. The depression came because I had suffered so greatly in my past and I'd never fully accepted or dealt with my true feelings about the deep hurts of my childhood. True depression is anger directed inward and there was so much anger inside me. It is not in my nature to hurt others because I have been hurt so horribly so the anger turned in. I pretended I was *okay* and forced myself to be strong. I smiled past the pain and pushed my feelings aside. I told myself lies like, I didn't really *need* a father, that I was *fine* without a mother, the fire of my childhood that *tried* to burn me, never actually burned me. I lied to myself that I walked away unscathed. I didn't want to "feel". I always stayed busy. To stop, was to feel. I was also diagnosed with PTSD brought on by the trauma from my childhood. I would have flashbacks and moments where it felt I was reliving that trauma. The PTSD made me super alert and forever scanning the environment for danger. I analyzed people too much because as a kid that skill kept me safe. It also kept me away from good people and healthy relationships. I was so used to the crisis that I didn't know what to do with myself when things were peaceful, and it felt impossible to stop being afraid all the time.

I thought feeling my true feelings about my childhood would *kill* me. I was allowed to be hurt, violated in my body and mind, and I endured isolation, neglect, and abuse. I didn't want to feel the rejection of my father or the neglect of my mother. I didn't want to feel the profound sadness that was within me as a result of my childhood. I lied about my *true* feelings, even to myself. *Feeling* all that was like reopening a wound. All of these falsehoods kept me thinking I was *truly* okay when really, I wasn't. You can tell if someone is okay based upon their level of happiness. Joy is a barometer. If we feel like life is always hard, or we are overly negative, aggressive, or cynical, that is pointing to something needing to change. My change was in my mind. It was in my thoughts, perceptions, and beliefs. I believed the world was a war zone because that was my world.

Questions came up in therapy such as: Why did I feel the need to always be strong all the time? Why did I permit abuse by setting no boundary to people's mistreatment? Why was I so careful at not letting others in and always scanning? Why couldn't I feel my feelings?

How do I really feel? Why do I hide my story? Why can't I just stop feeling afraid all the time? It took me years to truly show my real feelings because they were so guarded. I didn't give myself permission to reveal weakness. I never allowed myself a moment. There were many reasons for this. If I was weak, mom, like a shark would prey upon the blood in the water, and I would become her person to inflict pain upon. My armor helped me survive. I learned to pretend and to lie. If I fell apart, that made our entire house crumble. I felt that pressure *always to* hold it together and was not allowed the luxury of breaking emotionally. I needed to acknowledge that I had feelings about what had happened to me.

At thirty-four, I had the funeral and I let my heart open. I cried for the first time about my childhood. The tears flowed for nearly two weeks. That is how much I held inside. I allowed myself the space to feel the anger, the injustice, the sadness, the relief, the terror, the horror, and eventually the forgiveness and gratitude. There is no timeline for healing. We all heal at a different pace.

The first four sessions, the pain that was my childhood poured out of me in tears. Words couldn't capture the essence of how I felt, but tears could capture the feeling perfectly. I held it together for *so* long and finally, the levy broke. As I began to talk about things I had never *ever* intended to talk about, the ice surrounding my heart began to crack and to melt. It was like doing surgery. Thorns were being pulled out of my heart. The more I talked about it, the more I became okay with feeling it, and accepting everything. However, that first incision was brutal.

I had damaged scar tissue and infection and emotional surgery was necessary for me to revisit the wounds in order to move forward in my life. The unfelt feelings were like a blockage that was being unclogged from within my heart. It was ugly. Not everyone can handle your mess and be careful who you show your wounds to. Not everyone is a doctor. More life could eventually flow to my heart, but the pain of healing was not easy. Talking and feeling were painful. Allowing the gunk and buildup of my heart to flow out, was hard.

I finally learned that none of what happened to me was my doing. I was a victim. My mom was also a victim. I learned to give her compassion. She did the best she could.

I learned being born in crazy wasn't my identity. My story didn't make me any less of a person. I believed I was trash and I was trying to *prove* to everyone, no really, I'm worthy. I'm not what I came from. That's part of why I didn't reach toward Spiky. I believed I was less than. That deeply held belief and inability to open to him came back to having a damaged view of self. I believed I was not deserving of his effort. If I had a stronger sense of self, my home life wouldn't have been an issue because I would have been sure of *myself*. All of that needed rebuilt and was part of my renovation.

The strong perfectionist existing inside me constantly proved to the world my value. But actually, I already had value. Realizing that truth, helped me to love and honor myself. I let my true self out to play, not the afraid girl. I stopped hiding.

Deep down, that belief needed to be transformed and reborn into a better image of myself. Being born into a mess didn't make me a mistake. The painting that is my life is both beautiful and ugly. I grew in the small crack despite the heavy restraint and resistance. My environment wasn't conducive, and I had breaches in my development. Seeing this realization, and feeling my emotion about it, and having compassion toward myself helped me to accept and love myself.

Learning to be kind and compassionate to self comes with understanding. When you comprehend *why* you are the way you are, it empowers you to grow. In understanding myself, that empowered me. When you are expected to be ultra-responsible, you tend to be hard on yourself. I was my mother's caregiver. I was a mom to my sibling. I cooked and cleaned and made sure that everyone was okay all the time. I fixed messes and was on high alert. I always had a worry and weight on me feeling powerless over mom's illness. For the first time, I found myself feeling compassion toward myself because I understood myself.

I used to feel that if someone loved me hard enough, the holes which my parents created would be filled and that finally, I would be whole. I now know true love comes from within. Good parents are supposed to set that example of love, but I had to learn it by myself. I have all I need inside me. A man or a woman cannot heal you, only you can. My husband showed me, so gracefully, he would continue to love me while he replanted me and brought me out of that tiny crack in the cement, but I was the one who decided to grow. Choices change the trajectory of your life. I'm thankful for the many choices, but most of all for choosing him. Eyebrows knew my potential was being choked due to my surroundings. He saw value in me before I ever did. Once I was in a safe place, surrounded in love, my life grew immensely.

Allowing people, a safe place to heal is important. Allowing people to bleed for a while until their wounds close, is necessary. Don't rush healing. Nurses know this. No one heals the same. You can have two people with the same injury, and both will heal in their *own* way and in their *own* time.

Grieving is okay. Being angry is okay. Don't put a timeline on your emotions. When you are done feeling them, you will know. The problem comes when we suffocate our emotions; those unfelt emotions demand to be felt. They squirt out in other areas, whether that be overeating, drugs, pain, overwork, abuse, affairs, or perfectionism. Feeling feelings is not always pretty. Allowing skilled licensed credentialed providers to navigate you through difficult emotional terrain is important, especially with trauma. Give yourself a space to be authentically you. Don't sugar coat it or draw a curtain over it but expose and unveil the real you (in a safe place). Take off your armor and show your wounds. You will get out of therapy, what you put in.

Why did I write this book? What comes from the heart reaches the heart. I wanted to share my story of a person living up close and personal with mental illness. I hope to inspire others. I suppose everyone feels they suffer in life, but my childhood felt like a war zone. I came out swinging. I should not have made it out of that, in an

292

emotional or in a statistical sense. Getting out of dysfunction felt like an impossible climb.

Acceptance is not approval. Grace and forgiveness do not mean you grant access to someone with close proximity to your soul. Loving yourself enough to say no is important. I've seen the footprint and ubiquity of God all around my life.

Therapy glued me back together. It's been several years now of reckoning. I no longer feel sad when I talk about my past or feel responsible to track mom's illness. The soft spot in my heart for her is my greatest weakness and knowing that has helped *me* draw a boundary line for my own sanity. I am happy. I've dealt with it and don't need to visit there often. They're just scars now. But the story has deep meaning for me. For the first time ever, I'm able to come out of hiding and tell my true story with no shame. It is liberating to be exactly who you are.

There is something empowering about being able to own your trauma. There is freedom in being able to speak and be validated. It is understanding that my feelings were not wrong. Being able to state the immorality, helped to honor my experience and my feelings. Adversity is opportunity. Do what you believe is right and learn to speak your mind. None of us are impervious to criticism; it is part of the game of life. Trials are part of the ascent and the journey matures us. Reaching the summit isn't what life is about. I live in the moment and focus on being truly happy. Thank you to all the survivors who continue to press for healing. You will find it, keep going. If you suffer from a mental illness, there is no shame. Find help and there is a way for your life to be healed. Thank you to all the loved ones who keep loving people through their trauma and through their illness. It takes a special person to love a hurting soul. We must first feel love. After we feel loved, we can be transparent without fear. Transparency leads to acceptance. Acceptance leads to understanding.

Understanding leads to compassion. Eventually, there is

healing. Love changes everything.

ENDING

I want to thank my family for allowing me the space to go back in time and recall these personal events, so I could write this book. They gave up time with me, in order for me to write this. Going back brought emotions to the surface and my family certainly felt all of that. Getting in touch with my feelings helped me explore the complexity of my past that I feel was necessary to honoring my story. Revisiting my experience, allowed for magnification. I could see the situation anew, which allowed for compassion and insight. Emotions are life experiences that bring connections with other people. In being vulnerable, I found my tribe. I am thankful my family supported me in this journey because sharing my story was important to me. Thank you.

BIOGRAPHY

Growing up in Iowa in the 1980s, with a mentally ill mother helped shape Diana's perspective and experience around what it was like living with the chaos, pain, and confusion of mental illness. Being in love with books and writing her entire life, Diana went on to write about the agony and triumph of her experience in order to inspire others. She attended business school and is an avid outdoorsman who currently resides in Nevada. She loves to hike in the mountains and go camping with her husband, and daughter.

Made in the USA
Coppell, TX
20 April 2021